"Jennifer LeClaire has blessed th
revealing the real spirit of Jezebel.
book. It will enlighten and enable every believer to discern the spirit
of Jezebel and overcome its seductive goals of leading God's people
into sexual immorality and idolatry. God bless you, Jennifer, for having the courage to expose the Jezebel spirit."

Dr. Bill Hamon, bishop, Christian International
Ministries Network; author, *Prophets and Personal
Prophecy*, *Day of the Saints* and ten others

"Church trends come and go, but the principalities and powers we
wrestle with as the Body of Christ haven't changed for millennia. In her
latest book, Jennifer LeClaire exposes the timeless Jezebel spirit that
still deceives believers today into believing it is merely about control
and manipulation. By peeling back the layers of this seductive spirit,
Jennifer not only opens the eyes of unaware believers but equips them
for war. And having worked daily with Jennifer on the front lines of
media and ministry, I know few others as battle-tested as she is in
fighting this rampant force."

Marcus Yoars, editor, *Charisma*

"This book could not be more timely! Jennifer LeClaire, with prophetic
precision, magnifies and exposes the root causes and principalities
that would seduce and ultimately destroy the voice and authority
of the individual believer and the corporate Church. *The Spiritual
Warrior's Guide to Defeating Jezebel* will provoke you to an honest
review and equip you to be cloaked with God's authority through a
life of authenticity and holiness in Christ. Our private choices have
public consequences, yet those who will be honest with themselves
and hungry for truth will find the message of this book liberating and
victorious, not confining and defeating."

Doug Stringer, founder/president, Somebody Cares America/
International and Turning Point Ministries International, Houston

"Finally, a book that cuts through the husk, hype and hysteria surrounding Jezebel and its diabolical doctrine of sexual immorality.
Many have tried but failed to expose the real underlying error that

triggered such spiritual havoc in the church of Thyatira and continues throughout the Body of Christ to this day. Using her anointed pen and powerful prophetic voice, Jennifer LeClaire provides us with insight, wisdom and instruction on how to recognize and deal with this deadly and dangerous foe. An essential read for all spiritual leaders."

David Ravenhill, author and teacher

"In my own books I have confronted the Baal-driven culture of this world and the pervasive immorality and self-focus it breeds. Like a voice crying in the wilderness, Jennifer LeClaire echoes these concerns in powerful terms. I heartily endorse its message. Read it and pray for a new reformation."

R. Loren Sandford, senior pastor, New Song
Church and Ministries, Denver

"The story of Jezebel is timeless. The spirit that drove her drives multitudes today. It is obvious that Jennifer LeClaire has dealt with this spirit's treacherous tactics. As a watchman on the wall, Jennifer has been motivated to write this war manual. It should be in the hands of all who refer to themselves as 'spiritual warriors.' There are no wasted words, and there is no time to waste! According to the Word of God, 'The name of the wicked shall rot' (Proverbs 10:7). Jezebel's name has rotted, but her character continues to influence thousands of lives today. Let's devour this teaching and destroy the spirit once and for all."

Steve Hill, evangelist, Dallas

"A challenging, amazingly helpful, unusual book! Spiritual warriors gain new insights for empowerment and prayer. Using many eye-opening Scriptures, shocking illustrations and reliable resources, Jennifer LeClaire boldly unveils Jezebel and Babylon, master agents of the adversary who seeks to wreck society and destroy the Church. A masterful guide for counterattack."

Ernest Gentile, Ministers Fellowship International;
honorary member, Apostolic Leadership Team

THE SPIRITUAL WARRIOR'S GUIDE TO
DEFEATING JEZEBEL

THE SPIRITUAL WARRIOR'S GUIDE TO
DEFEATING JEZEBEL

HOW TO OVERCOME THE SPIRIT OF CONTROL, IDOLATRY AND IMMORALITY

Jennifer LeClaire

Chosen

a division of Baker Publishing Group
Minneapolis, Minnesota

© 2013 by Jennifer LeClaire

Published by Chosen Books
11400 Hampshire Avenue South
Bloomington, Minnesota 55438
www.chosenbooks.com

Chosen Books is a division of
Baker Publishing Group, Grand Rapids, Michigan

Printed in the United States of America

Library of Congress Cataloging-in-Publication Data
LeClaire, Jennifer (Jennifer L.)
     The spiritual warrior's guide to defeating Jezebel : how to overcome the spirit of control, idolatry and immorality / Jennifer LeClaire ; Foreword by Mike Bickle.
        pages cm
     Summary: "*Charisma* magazine news editor and prophetic voice exposes the overlooked manifestations of the Jezebel spirit and reveals vital information on how to overcome this murderous evil"—Provided by publisher.
     ISBN 978-0-8007-9541-2 (pbk. : alk. paper)
     1. Jezebel, Queen, consort of Ahab, King of Israel. 2. Spiritual warfare. I. Title.
BS580.J45L43 2013
235'.4—dc23   2013002787

Cover design by Lookout Design, Inc.

13 14 15 16 17 18 19   7 6 5 4 3 2 1

This book is dedicated to my daughter, Bridgette, whose wisdom and discernment exceed her years and whose heart for global missions inspires me.

Contents

Foreword

The spirit of Jezebel is operating in the Church—but many do not understand it. In the early Church, Jesus taught that Jezebel tempted believers to tolerate and promote idolatry and immorality among the saints (see Revelation 2:20–21).

Yet some today see this serious problem as merely a woman with a strong personality who tries to manipulate and control people. If we limit our understanding of Jezebel to this, then we will miss what Jesus was saying.

In *The Spiritual Warrior's Guide to Defeating Jezebel*, Jennifer LeClaire sounds an alarm about the danger of this in the end time Church. Jennifer shows us in Scripture how Jezebel is more than just control and manipulation.

In essence, Jezebel is a spirit of seduction. Jennifer is lifting her voice against an ever-increasing demonic invasion in the Church called immorality. She exposes the roots of the Jezebel spirit and offers practical examples of how distorted teachings on the grace of God are allowing this seductive power to have its way in the Church.

Scripture is clear: Because of His great love for His people, Jesus will confront and judge those who refuse to repent of the idolatry and immorality that Jezebel participated in (see Revelation 2:22–23). However, He promised power over the nations to those who overcome her. Jennifer equips readers with the truth you need to overcome so you can maintain an intimate relationship with Jesus and reign with Him in eternity.

Mike Bickle,
director of the International
House of Prayer–Kansas City

Acknowledgments

First, I want to express my deepest appreciation to Jane Campbell, editorial director of Chosen Books, for being willing to consider publishing a work about the dangerous aspects of Jezebel that go beyond the popular understanding of this principality.

Also, many thanks to Mike Bickle, director of the International House of Prayer in Kansas City, whose teachings on Jezebel inspired me to dig beyond the stereotypes that have blanketed this spirit and root out the truth of just how wicked this end time enemy really is.

Last, but not least, I bless those who persecuted me so sorely that it motivated me to search for deeper truth about Jezebel and expose the underlying motives of this spirit. It is my prayer that the information offered here will help others not be tempted into making false accusations against the innocent while the real enemy goes unnoticed.

1

The Jezebel Deception

The Jezebel deception. It sounds like an intriguing murder mystery that promises to hold you in suspense right until the last page of the book—and indeed it is. You have learned about this crafty villain, perhaps in sermons, and have read warnings in Scripture. You might even be sure that you have seen it in your own church. You continue to gather clues to help you uncover the true identity of "Jezebel," but, as we will soon discover, it is likely that you have been sidetracked—or even duped—by red herrings along the way. This is not an insignificant enemy.

Like all captivating murder mysteries, the Jezebel deception presents a sinister antagonist. The antagonist in this story is, of course, a spiritual seductress named Jezebel. Her victims are real—the countless saints this siren has lulled into destruction. And the uncompromising protagonist who stands ready to set the captives free from the sorceress is none other than the Lord Jesus Christ.

Jezebel's fate is sealed, and so are the fates of her spiritual children—those who follow her teaching. Yet despite decades of teaching about Jezebel—and despite the fact that the book of Revelation outlines its motives and tactics and even shows the way of escape—many in the Body of Christ seem ignorant as to who Jezebel really is, how it manifests, and how to overcome this ancient foe.

That is because Jezebel hides its most malevolent actions behind the mask of control and manipulation—characteristics that do not always demand the gift of discerning of spirits to identify—and these are the traits on which most "Jezebel" sermons focus.

The result: Christians are whacking away in prayer at superficial fruit while the root that feeds Jezebel grows stronger and manifests more and more powerfully. Most people are clueless, not recognizing the subtle work and hidden motives of this spiritual being; they fail to investigate below the surface to see the demonic roots and the deeper agenda. Control and manipulation are strong manifestations, but ultimately they are merely means to an end.

Jezebel's Greatest Deception

Nineteenth-century French poet Charles Baudelaire once said that Satan's greatest deception is convincing the world he does not exist. If that is true, then perhaps Jezebel's greatest deception is convincing the Church that it is nothing more than the spirit of control. Think about it. If your enemy can distract you from his purpose by throwing out false clues as to where he is hiding, then he can catch you off guard, ambush you and take you captive. That is just what Jezebel is doing by convincing the Church that its motive is nothing more than to control and manipulate for the sake of power and authority.

The strategy is working. Online stores offer books and videos by the hundreds proclaiming Jezebel to be the "spirit of control" and suggesting ways to break, overthrow, defeat and otherwise expose the spirit of Jezebel. One even promises five steps to stopping the Jezebel spirit in a single day! Jezebel must be laughing out loud as people battle against the wrong spirit.

Jezebel has become marketable, a demonic superstar that draws attention from some spiritual warfare camps intent on putting this spirit of control under their feet or pulling down its influence over cities once and for all. Indeed, Jezebel has become such a key topic that Christians are penning novels about it. Some pastors have jumped on the Jezebel bandwagon, attracting visitors to their websites with little understanding of what they are really dealing with. These shepherds are unknowingly propagating the Jezebel deception. The spirit of Jezebel must be relishing the attention—and the reality that it is keeping the deeper danger well hidden.

Jezebel's greatest deception is convincing Spirit-filled churchgoers that it is a power-hungry, self-promoting spirit of control that wants to cozy up to the pastor in order to gain a position of spiritual authority in the local church. This is partly true: Jezebel manifests with control and manipulation. But that is merely the low-hanging fruit of a rotten tree.

Jezebel has succeeded in distracting the Church from its broader purpose by disguising what it really is—a spirit of seduction that leads people into immorality and idolatry (see Revelation 2:20) and a partner with Babylon that seeks to murder. The Lady of the Kingdoms brags, "No one sees me" (Isaiah 47:10). The Lady of the Kingdoms is the spirit of Babylon and its religious running mate is Jezebel. Part of Jezebel's agenda is to seduce people to worship the Lady of the Kingdoms instead of the King of kings. It may begin with control and manipulation, but it ends in murder.

Rev 2:20
Is 47:10

Principality, Power or Spirit?

Before we look more closely at the Jezebel deception, let's get on the same page about certain terminology. Some in charismatic circles like to say you have to "separate the principality from the personality" when you deal with difficult people. That is another way of saying we should hate the sin and love the sinner.

Jesus still loves sinners who might succumb to a Jezebel spirit, and He offers them repentance, but Scripture makes clear that "the LORD hates . . . a proud look, a lying tongue, hands that shed innocent blood, a heart that devises wicked plans, feet that are swift in running to evil, a false witness who speaks lies, and one who sows discord among brethren" (Proverbs 6:16–19). Jezebel is an active participant in these and other sins—as are the individuals she controls.

Where does Jezebel fall in the apostle Paul's hierarchy of the demonic in Ephesians 6? Paul said by the inspiration of the Holy Spirit that we need to put on the whole armor of God. There is a good reason for this exhortation—we are wrestling "against principalities, against powers, against the rulers of the darkness of this age, against spiritual hosts of wickedness in the heavenly places" (Ephesians 6:12). Is Jezebel a principality, a power, a ruler of the darkness of this age? Is Jezebel a garden-variety spirit or demon or devil?

There is disagreement in the Body of Christ about where Jezebel (and other spirits, for that matter) falls in the Ephesians 6 listing. The word *principality* comes from the Greek word *arché*, which means "chief or ruler." It suggests authority or rule in the world. From the modern English dictionary, we learn that principalities rule over jurisdictions. They are "princes" of territories. If you look at certain regions of the world, you will see the influence of principalities.

For our discussion, and to avoid confusion, we will use *devil* to refer to Satan himself, and *demon* for a lower level spirit. It seems

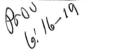

logical to view Jezebel near the top in the hierarchy, perhaps a principality, though it is best known as the "spirit of Jezebel."

Although Jezebel wields weapons of control and manipulation, Jezebel is *not* the spirit of control. Jezebel is essentially the spirit of seduction. Jezebel works to seduce us into immorality and idolatry.

Jesus spoke clearly to the church of Thyatira: "Nevertheless, I have this against you: You tolerate that woman Jezebel, who calls herself a prophet. By her teaching she misleads my servants into sexual immorality and the eating of food sacrificed to idols" (Revelation 2:20, NIV). So while the church is intent on shunning assertive people and sewing an imaginary scarlet letter on the blouses of women with overbearing personalities, we are allowing the real principality to have its way in the pulpit and the pews. We are tolerating that woman Jezebel. We are violating Scripture.

Where there is no repentance, immorality eventually sears the conscience. We are no longer sensitive to the Spirit of God, yet we long for spiritual encounters. That is where the spirit of idolatry comes in. Compromised believers seek supernatural experiences and sometimes encounter demonic manifestations and visitations. They claim this is the Holy Ghost, but it is not the Holy Ghost. It is an "angel of light" that ushers them into greater deception.

That Woman Jezebel

The Jezebel deception is an age-old script that runs through biblical history. We read in 2 Kings 9:34 that Jehu confronted Queen Jezebel—the wife of Israel's King Ahab—and called her "accursed." While exiled on the isle of Patmos, John the apostle recorded a revelation of Jesus Christ, in which Jesus confronted "that woman" Jezebel (Revelation 2:22). Those are not the only two manifestations of the Jezebel spirit we find in

2Kings 9:34
Rev 2:22

Scripture. We can see Jezebel working in the lives of Samson, David, Solomon and others. And we see Jezebel working in the lives of prominent figures in the Church today.

In Revelation 2:22–23, Jesus promised to cast the false prophetess Jezebel into a "sickbed" and "kill her children with death." Harsh words from a loving Savior—and that should give you the first clue as to just how wicked this spirit really is. Jesus was not dealing with a controlling, manipulative woman who refused to submit to the pastor. Jesus was addressing the veiled and evil purpose of Jezebel: murder.

In order to understand the depths of the Jezebel deception, one must understand the spirit that motivated the biblical characters known as Jezebel. The spirit of Jezebel existed long before the queen described in 1 Kings and the false prophetess introduced in Revelation. When you understand the true motive of this spirit, you will see that it was alive and well way back in the age of Nimrod, centuries earlier.

We will dive deeper into this history in chapter 4, but I want to say a word here about the person most Bible students associate with the spirit of Jezebel, and that is the evil woman who became queen. Queen Jezebel so personified the spirit of Jezebel that this is what we call it.

Jezebel was a Phoenician princess who married Ahab, king of Israel. Her father was Ethbaal, king and high priest of the Sidonians. Queen Jezebel introduced Baal worship into Israel. By acquiescing to her idolatry, King Ahab broke the first two commandments:

> "You shall have no other gods before Me. You shall not make for yourself a carved image—any likeness of anything that is in heaven above, or that is in the earth beneath, or that is in the water under the earth; you shall not bow down to them nor serve them."
>
> Exodus 20:3–5

Baal worship gives us clues as to the workings of Jezebel. The name *Baal* means "lord" or "possessor." According to the *Dake Annotated Reference Bible*, Baal is the sun-god of Phoenicia, and the supreme deity among the Canaanites and various other pagan nations. His full title is *Baal-Shemaim*, which means "lord of heaven." In Greek mythology, Baal is the equivalent of Zeus.

The Canaanites, who were Baal worshipers, participated in sex worship, fertility rites, religious prostitution and human sacrifice—all to pacify the gods. Fast-forward 54 chapters in the Bible and you find the false prophetess Jezebel who teaches and seduces God's servants to commit sexual immorality and eat things sacrificed to idols. Can you see the stage being set for idolatry and sexual immorality in Jezebel's world? Where Jezebel is pulling the strings, you will find idolatry and sexual immorality behind the curtain.

Just how sinister is the Jezebel spirit? *Easton's Bible Dictionary* says,

> Jezebel has stamped her name on history as the representative of all that is designing, crafty, malicious, revengeful and cruel. She is the first great instigator of persecution against the saints of God. Guided by no principle, restrained by no fear of either God or man, passionate in her attachment to her heathen worship, she spared no pains to maintain idolatry around her in all its splendor.

Matthew Henry's *Commentary* calls Jezebel a "zealous idolater, extremely imperious and malicious in her natural temper, addicted to witchcrafts and whoredoms, and every way vicious."

Clearly, the spirit of Jezebel is interested in more than control and manipulation. We have to discern the deeper motive of this spirit if we ever hope to resist the temptations that will lead to the great falling away that Paul writes about in 2 Thessalonians 2:3. Jude urges us to contend earnestly for the faith once delivered to us, because "certain men have crept in unnoticed . . .

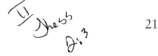

21

ungodly men, who turn the grace of our God into lewdness and deny the only Lord God and our Lord Jesus Christ" (Jude 4).

The spirit of Jezebel is already running rampant in the world. Unfortunately, Jezebel is also running loose in the Church and manifests in many local congregations without anyone ever seeing it—or confronting it.

Jezebel Goes to Church

If Jezebel is not a spirit of control and manipulation, what, then, does Jezebel look like? It looks just the way many books describe—on the surface. This is why so many are deceived. Jezebel is not merely a woman (or a man) with an overbearing personality or immature character. Jezebel's influence runs much deeper than a desire to make someone a mouthpiece or puppet, or control the worship song list, or intimidate people from joining the inner circle in order to guard the leadership positions of those it controls.

Let's be real. Some of those bossy, controlling people just need to read *How to Win Friends and Influence People* and they would be fine. In other words, some saints just need good old-fashioned people skills.

So, think again: What does Jezebel look like in the Church? Male or female, a Jezebelite—meaning a person who is influenced or dominated by this spirit—is a subtle seducer. And the key word is *subtle*. If Jezebel was obvious no one would be fooled. A Jezebelite usually has a charismatic personality that draws people to other gods and away from Christ. Sometimes she succeeds in this idolatry by exalting pastors—puffing them up, putting them on a pedestal, giving them the honor God should have. She also does this by luring people to the things of the world, and by introducing doctrines and principles that sound godly but come from the world's system.

Example

Likewise, a Jezebelite is quick to encourage sin. A woman confides in her, for instance, that she is having sex out of wedlock. The Jezebelite will assure the woman that it is okay if she is in love, easing the guilt and glossing over any godly conviction the woman might feel.

Please hear me: If we look only for control and manipulation, we will wrongly accuse people of "flowing in a Jezebel spirit," while the principality wreaks havoc in the lives of people in the Church.

Jezebel's Hatred for Prophets

There have been strong lines drawn between God's prophets and Jezebel. Remember, it was the wicked Queen Jezebel who is credited with killing the Lord's prophets. Obadiah risked his life by hiding a hundred prophets in two caves and feeding them bread and water, while Jezebel's own prophets sat at a table overflowing with rich food and wine (see 1 Kings 18:4, 19). From this contrast we see there are carnal rewards for cooperating with Jezebel in this lifetime, and there are eternal rewards for refusing to tolerate that spirit.

By the same token, God will not wait until eternity to pour out judgments on those who refuse to repent of flowing in a Jezebel spirit. Nor will those who refuse to tolerate that spirit go unrewarded in this lifetime. I can tell you this from experience. If you refuse to bow down to Jezebel—no matter what it costs you—God will repay you, at least in part, even now. Indeed, I believe the very fact that I am writing this book is God's reward to me for standing up to that spirit.

Jezebel targets prophetic voices because it wants to shut down the voice of God to make room for false prophetic utterance, which promotes immoral, idolatrous religion. Although some teachings draw a connection solely between Jezebel and

1 Kings 19
18:1

the prophets, Jezebel is not after prophets alone. If saints believe that Jezebel is only after the prophets—or the pastors, or other leaders in the Body—they will put down their guard and become easy prey. In other words, if they are not spiritual leaders they feel no need to be concerned about Jezebel targeting them.

Jezebel will gladly control, manipulate and work through any hurt, wounded or willing vessel. Never think you are immune to Jezebel's agenda just because you are not particularly prophetic. You might not hold the office of prophet, but if you have been filled with the Holy Spirit you have the gift of prophecy. And even if you have never sought to be "Spirit-filled," Jezebel will do its dirty work through you if you will let it.

That said, Jezebel considers prophetic voices a strategic investment. If Jezebel can shut down or pervert the voice of a spiritual leader it can influence religious culture. When that happens, we witness the rise of prophetic puppets for Jezebel instead of the rise of prophetic pioneers for Jesus. Instead of pure vessels who speak what the Spirit of God says, we have warped warriors for a seducing goddess bent on leading people into the bondage of sexual immorality and idolatry.

Are You Armed for Battle?

Right now, we are witnessing Jezebel both perverting and making puppets out of prophets at the same time. I believe a showdown lies ahead. Jehovah wants you to serve Him with all your heart, all your soul and all your strength. Jezebel wants your devotion, too. The difference is, Jesus will not manipulate you into serving Him. The Holy Spirit will never try to control you. Jezebel will. All of us come to a time in our lives when we reach the Valley of Shechem. The Lord is saying to you, "Choose this day whom you will serve" (see Joshua 24:15).

Sadly, much of the Church is completely ignorant of this war in the heavens—and much of the Church is fighting the spirit of control thinking it is Jezebel. This deception must not continue. We must stop being distracted by the red herrings that divert us from the truth. Jesus promises authority over nations to those who conquer Jezebel—and judgment to those who follow Jezebel's false doctrine.

Since many Christian leaders do not understand the deeper danger of the Jezebel spirit, few are working to equip the saints with truth to combat its wicked strategy. Let's face it: Jezebel is a topic that draws a crowd and sells books. But, again, Satan is probably sitting back laughing as we continue to produce incomplete teaching on the subject of Jezebel that keeps the Lady of the Kingdoms hidden from our view.

Yes, Babylon and the spirit of Jezebel will one day fall in judgment. But so will all those unrepentant people Jezebel has seduced into idolatry and immorality. We should be warring against this! Armed with a fuller understanding of what Jezebel really is, we can avoid falling into its trap through misguided teachings on grace or plain ignorance of this principality's devices. Armed with the truth, you can walk free from the sinful influences of Jezebel. But you need the whole truth. . . .

2

A Royal Rebuke

The Church is always shocked when her high-profile leaders are exposed in sexual immorality—and so it should be. We expect to follow their example as they follow Christ's example (see 1 Corinthians 11:1). Tragically, too many have followed Jezebel instead. Whether it is adulterous affairs, homosexuality confessions or child molestation charges, the saints usually never saw the impending fall of their beloved leaders and are devastated when confronted with the sordid details.

Why did they not see it coming? It seems a number of scandal-rocked churches were having major, positive impact before the disclosure was shouted from the rooftops.

Jesus said, "You will know them by their fruits" (Matthew 7:16). But let's remember that Jesus also said, "There is nothing covered that will not be revealed, and hidden that will not be known" (Matthew 10:26). God is long-suffering, but eventually the proud fall if they do not repent (see Proverbs 16:18). When Christian leaders start making newspaper headlines for *causing* instead of *relieving* suffering, it damages the faith of many saints who believed they were sowing their time, money and very lives into a righteous ministry.

Despite the rash of horrifying headlines, scandal-rocked churches are not a recent phenomenon in the Body of Christ. The New Testament offers examples of congregations where sexual immorality was running rampant. Two that come immediately to mind are the church at Corinth and the church at Thyatira. Both churches had strong attributes, yet both met with rebuke.

Indeed, the church at Corinth was flowing in spiritual gifts; authentic miracles were taking place. Yet Paul rebuked the church for making idols out of men: "Now I say this, that each of you says, 'I am of Paul,' or 'I am of Apollos,' or 'I am of Cephas,' or 'I am of Christ.' Is Christ divided? Was Paul crucified for you? Or were you baptized in the name of Paul?" (1 Corinthians 1:12–13).

He also rebuked them for allowing sexual immorality in their midst:

> It is actually reported that there is sexual immorality among you, and such sexual immorality as is not even named among the Gentiles—that a man has his father's wife! And you are puffed up, and have not rather mourned, that he who has done this deed might be taken away from among you.
>
> 1 Corinthians 5:1–2

The church at Thyatira was also making a positive mark on its surrounding community. In fact, the church at Thyatira had a reputation for its good works, love, faith and patience. In these churches, we see both the gifts of the Holy Spirit and the fruit of the Holy Spirit manifesting even in an environment where Jezebel was seducing the saints. This tells us that signs, wonders and miracles do not necessarily mean that a church is healthy.

From the outside looking in, the Thyatira ministry made a good first impression. As for works of service, Jesus said this body of believers was increasing in its outreach. Many in this church loved the Lord and were deeply committed to sharing the Gospel. At first blush, this sounds like a church that world changers and history makers would love to attend. It sounds like the Church being the Church. Yet after heaping praise on this congregation, Jesus issued one of the strongest rebukes found in the New Testament. Let's listen in:

> "I know your works, love, service, faith, and your patience; and as for your works, the last are more than the first. Nevertheless I have a few things against you, because you allow that woman Jezebel, who calls herself a prophetess, to teach and seduce My servants to commit sexual immorality and eat things sacrificed to idols."
>
> Revelation 2:19–20

Charismatic Adulterers

Jesus appreciated this local church's outreach, but this meek One who is lowly in heart rose up with righteous indignation at leadership allowing an influential false prophetess to teach doctrine that put a stamp of approval on immorality and idolatry. Rather than confronting believers who abused the grace of God by practicing these lifestyles—and instead of working with the Holy Spirit to lead them gently back to the right path—leadership put up with this compromise. They tolerated compromise, and it opened their minds to deadly deception. The pastors at the Thyatira church essentially allowed members of the Body to become slaves to sin from which Jesus died to free them. Truly, it was a travesty of justice in the eyes of a just God.

Let's focus for a moment on the aspect of sexual immorality in this church. Although the church at Thyatira was fruitful in

29

many ways, a spiritual death spread from within because leadership turned a blind eye to sin. How did it happen? Maybe it was because the adulterers in the church had the most charismatic preaching and teaching gifts. Maybe the homosexuals contributed the largest offerings for the new building project. Maybe the fornicators were the most skilled minstrels.

Those statements may shock you, but I have watched this play out. Concerns begin to be voiced about a young worship singer having sexual encounters with a married man (or an unbeliever or even the youth pastor). Leadership turns a blind eye to the accusations from two, three and more witnesses—and reprimands the ones bringing the truthful charges—because the singer draws a crowd. — How does this play out in our lives?

Too often, it is only when the young woman is visibly pregnant that fornicators are expelled from the public platform. The 21st-century Church is often willing to overlook sin because a person's gifts are bringing increase to a ministry. And this spiritual cancer called sexual immorality is metastasizing across many parts of the Body today. — The Bowling Family - It spreads

Paul warned the church at Corinth—and the Church at large—not to keep company with sexually immoral people (see 1 Corinthians 5:9). He exhorted us that the body is not for sexual immorality but for the Lord (see 1 Corinthians 6:13). He warned us to flee sexual immorality, which is a sin against one's own body (see 1 Corinthians 6:18). And Jude reminds us of Sodom and Gomorrah, whose inhabitants gave themselves over to sexual immorality and will suffer the vengeance of eternal fire (see Jude 7).

Open your eyes and look around you. A discerning spirit will discover that immorality is tolerated in local churches and large ministries alike. Just as Paul expected the leaders in the church at Corinth to confront the sexual immorality in their midst, so does Jesus expect leaders in the church today to do the same.

Look what happened to Eli when he refused to deal with the sexual immorality his sons were wallowing in (see 1 Samuel 2:12; 3:11–13). Just because a church is flowing and growing does not mean that it is healthy. *Stop & pray for our church & leaders*

Immorality's Cunning

Jesus said that Jezebel teaches God's servants to commit sexual immorality. No one is immune. Some who fall prey to Jezebel's seduction are new believers who are truly ignorant of the will of the Lord—or in deep bondage to the sinful flesh. They are saved by God's grace, but perhaps they do not immediately change their sinful ways. These new believers need the guidance of pastors who can offer godly, loving counsel and teachers who can expound on the Word of God in areas of sexual conduct and boundaries. Some may also need prophetic ministry to break demonic strongholds. The five-fold ministry is vital to raising up mature believers (see Ephesians 4:11–13). *New Believer* *the - important Scripture*

Others whom Jezebel solicits successfully are Christians looking for ways to justify their self-will—sometimes with the Word of God as a backstop. You can find many of these carnal believers penning articles for the Internet. Some of them insist sex is acceptable in God's eyes if a couple is engaged. They often point to Mary and Joseph. Mary was betrothed (engaged) to Joseph, who considered divorcing her privately when she was found to be pregnant (see Matthew 1:19). Based on this example, they reason, a commitment to marry annuls God's decision against sex before marriage. Not so! *← Joseph knew it wasn't his baby. How?*

Meanwhile, others draw broad lines around the definition of sexual immorality, suggesting that fondling and oral sex outside the bonds of marriage is within the acceptable boundaries of God's Word. This type of information merely sets up believers for a devastating fall by beguiling them into walking a tightrope *flee!!*

31

that spans the pit of Jezebel. Let's be clear: Sexual immorality is any sexual act outside of the covenant of marriage. Any sexual act.

Finally, Jezebel sometimes strings along even the most seasoned Christians. Jezebel often does this by hooking into their erroneous revelations of God's grace, which overshadow a healthy fear of the Lord. Thank God for His grace! It is true that where sin abounds, grace does more abound (see Romans 5:20). But does that give us a license to sin? "Shall we continue in sin that grace may abound? Certainly not! How shall we who died to sin live any longer in it?" (Romans 6:1–2).

I like the way *The Message* translates those verses:

> So what do we do? Keep on sinning so God can keep on forgiving? I should hope not! If we've left the country where sin is sovereign, how can we still live in our old house there? Or didn't you realize we packed up and left there for good?

When the Preacher Falls

Here is the point: Like all false teaching, the Jezebel deception is subtle. Few blood-bought, Bible-believing, Spirit-filled, tongue-talking Christians would voluntarily open wide and swallow a sermon that sanctioned pornography, fornication, homosexuality, adultery—or any other sexual immorality.

No, God's people love what He loves and hate what He hates, at least in theory (see Psalm 97:10). In fact, some who have fallen headlong into sexual immorality are among those who preached the most vehemently against it. Rather than rehashing well-known church scandals of recent years here, let's consider how the wisest man who ever lived fell into immorality: King Solomon.

Before he bowed a knee to sexual immorality, King Solomon preached through his Spirit-inspired proverbs about a type of

Jezebel. He described her as a loose woman who flatters with smooth words, one who searches for victims void of good sense and seduces them. (Read: Common sense will take you a long way toward avoiding Jezebel's sex trap.) Solomon was well aware of the dangers of sexual immorality and idolatry, as we learn in this passage:

> With much justifying and enticing argument she persuades him, with the allurements of her lips she leads him [to overcome his conscience and his fears] and forces him along. Suddenly he [yields and] follows her reluctantly like an ox moving to the slaughter, like one in fetters going to the correction [to be given] to a fool or like a dog enticed by food to the muzzle. Till a dart [of passion] pierces and inflames his vitals; then like a bird fluttering straight into the net [he hastens], not knowing that it will cost him his life.
>
> Proverbs 7:21–23, AMPLIFIED

How prophetic! Solomon's fall into immorality and idolatry did indeed cost him his life in God—but the "fall" did not happen overnight. It never does. People have to make a series of conscious decisions along the road to sexual immorality, reasoning away the reality of sin and relying on God's grace to be there when they are finished pursuing their fleshly desires. Again, Jezebel's deception is subtle. And this spirit is long-suffering. Jezebel, if it needs to, will probe a believer's heart for years looking for any area of weakness, any area that is not fully submitted to God.

King David fell into sexual immorality with Bathsheba, repented and continued walking in integrity for the rest of his life. He remains known as a man after God's own heart (see 1 Samuel 13:14). By contrast, Solomon multiplied his father's mistake many times over by repeatedly breaking God's Law. He practiced a sinful lifestyle, despite being blessed as the wisest

33

man in the world. That Solomon could fall from such great heights illustrates the danger of ignoring God's wisdom—and it should put the fear of God into every one of us. God has warned us about Jezebel because He loves us passionately and does not want to see us fall into this deadly trap. Let's look more closely at the tragic case of this mighty king.

Solomon's Sins Multiplied

God laid down the Law for kings in Deuteronomy 17:14–20. Kings were commanded not to multiply horses for themselves or cause the people to return to Egypt to multiply horses, yet the Bible records that Solomon's stock and trade in horses from Egypt was significant (see 1 Kings 10:26, 28–29). Kings were commanded not to multiply silver and gold for themselves, yet Solomon stockpiled enormous amounts of these precious metals (see 1 Kings 10:14–23). And, finally, kings were commanded not to multiply wives for themselves, lest their hearts be turned away from God, yet Solomon had seven hundred wives and three hundred concubines (see 1 Kings 11:1–3).

Some describe Solomon's temptations as wealth, weapons and women. The women were what ultimately did him in. And the saddest part was that he knew better. Jezebel's captivating charm swept him off his wise feet. Jezebel, also known as Ashtoreth, deceived the wisest man in the world. Let's recall the Bible account of Solomon's demise:

> King Solomon, however, loved many foreign women besides Pharaoh's daughter—Moabites, Ammonites, Edomites, Sidonians and Hittites. They were from nations about which the LORD had told the Israelites, "You must not intermarry with them, because they will surely turn your hearts after their gods." Nevertheless, Solomon held fast to them in love. He had seven hundred wives of royal birth and three hundred concubines, and

34

his wives led him astray. As Solomon grew old, his wives turned his heart after other gods, and his heart was not fully devoted to the LORD his God, as the heart of David his father had been. He followed Ashtoreth the goddess of the Sidonians, and Molek the detestable god of the Ammonites. So Solomon did evil in the eyes of the LORD; he did not follow the LORD completely, as David his father had done.

1 Kings 11:1–6, NIV

The story spirals downward from here. Solomon openly defied God by building a sacred shrine to Chemosh, the wicked god of Moab, and to Molek, the wicked god of the Ammonites. He also built shrines for all his foreign wives, who then polluted the countryside with the smoke and stench of their sacrifices. God was furious with Solomon, of course, for turning his back on their relationship in order to pursue immorality and idolatry (see 1 Kings 11:9–10). As with Saul, God informed Solomon that he would rip the kingdom from his hands and give it to another after his death. From that time on, God raised up adversaries against Solomon, and he lived in warfare. — where are we now?

This disturbing account sometimes causes me to ponder what is really going on inside ministries that live in constant spiritual warfare. I will be the first to admit that apostolic and prophetic ministries seem to get more than their "fair share" of spiritual warfare. Believe me. I totally understand. It sometimes feels as though the warfare never ends. But some ministries hold up the "We're under attack!" banner like a badge of honor that proves they are more important, more of a threat to the enemy or more dedicated to the cause of Christ than other ministries. It is a subtle insinuation, but it is there. And it is pride. It is idolatry.

I have been involved in these types of ministries in the past. Instead of examining ourselves to see if we were opening a door wide to the enemy, we preached, prayed and prophesied about warfare. We forgot that worship, too, is warfare, and we fell into the ditch of imbalance with a hyperactive focus on demons. I thank God He delivered me from that mind-set. Let us remember that even David, a man of war, had seasons of rest. The Bible assures us that there is a time for war, but also a time for peace (see Ecclesiastes 3:8).

I am not suggesting that every ministry that faces tremendous spiritual warfare is yielding to the spirit of Jezebel. Nor am I suggesting that some ministries have less intense warfare than others by nature of their calling. We are indeed in a war and the battle is fierce. But I do believe it is impossible to defeat what you are willingly submitting to. In other words, you cannot defeat the devil if you are submitting to the devil. You cannot defeat Jezebel if you are not willing to resist Jezebel's seductions. The Bible is clear about this: "Submit to God. Resist the devil and he will flee from you" (James 4:7). Yes, demons will come back to harass you again, but you will record a victory first.

Perverted, Bloodthirsty Gods

When Solomon blatantly and continually turned his heart from God, the constant warfare began. In other words, when Solomon turned his heart toward idols, he opened the door to warfare. Idols are actually demons (see 1 Corinthians 10:18–22).

The Bible says that Solomon was following after and even building altars to these other gods, to these idols. Who were these other gods? By understanding the nature of these demons we can better understand Jezebel and other spiritual forces at work that lead even the wisest, most God-fearing men and women into immorality and idolatry.

The Bible says that Solomon followed Ashtoreth the goddess of the Sidonians, and Molek the detestable god of the Ammonites. A look at these demons also helps us understand how idolatry and sexual immorality are connected.

36

Ashtoreth is the principal goddess of Canaan, also known as the wife of Baal and the Queen of Heaven. Ashtoreth is the very goddess that Israel worshiped during its times of apostasy (see Judges 2:13; 1 Samuel 7:3–4; 2 Kings 23:13). Ashtoreth is the goddess of love and war, and the chief god that Queen Jezebel served. As we noted earlier, Jezebel's father, Ethbaal, was the high priest of the goddess Ashtoreth.

Ashtoreth's priests, known in history as Gallis, were the male cult prostitutes mentioned in 1 Kings 14:24. Some historians believe them to have been eunuchs in women's attire.

Female devotees were prostitutes for the male devotees whose lustful orgies formed the main part of the worship. This worship was carried on in shrines, gardens and high places. Solomon married women who served Ashtoreth, and built temples where worship was reduced to sexual immorality. This is the immoral, idolatrous fruit of the spirit of Jezebel. You can see the homosexual connection in the eunuchs who dressed like women. You can see the sex trafficking of women. And you can see the spirit of lust in full operation.

Solomon also honored Molek. In an act that was an abomination to the Lord, people sacrificed their sons and daughters to Molek as an expression of devotion (see Jeremiah 32:35).

Some theologians connect abortion today to the bloodthirsty god of Molek, indicating that an unwanted pregnancy that ends with the child's death is, arguably, a sacrifice to this demon. Put another way, those who follow Ashtoreth partner with this demon named Molek to avoid the consequences of sexual sin or to maintain certain conveniences. They are selfish. They want sexual gratification, but they are not willing to carry, give birth to and raise the child. So they abort the child and resume life as usual, often to repeat the same sexual sin and the same murder.

After the life of an unborn child has been sacrificed, other demons harass and even oppress those who have chosen abortion.

[handwritten marginalia: Sex & murder]

[handwritten notes at bottom: Judges 2:13 / I Sam 7:3-4 / 2 Kings 23:13 / I Kings 14:24 — / Jer 32:35]

Depression. Alcohol abuse. Suicidal behaviors. These are a few of the mental health problems researchers are tying to abortion. A study entitled "Abortion and Mental Health: Quantitative Synthesis and Analysis of Research Published 1995–2009," by Priscilla Coleman, Ph.D., reveals that 81 percent of females who had an abortion were found to be at an increased risk for mental health problems.

Take figures for the year 2007. The Centers for Disease Control in the United States reports that 827,609 legal, induced abortions took place in the United States, and 84 percent of them were performed on unmarried women. The Guttmacher Institute reports that 47 percent of women who have abortions had at least one previous abortion. The instance of abortion among those who consider themselves Christians is shocking. Thirty-seven percent of women obtaining abortions identify themselves as Protestant and 28 percent as Catholic, according to the Guttmacher study. These women claim to serve God but most are deceived into following Ashtoreth and Molek in their decision.

Abusing Sexual Intimacy

As with Solomon, believers today fall prey to Jezebel's idolatry and sexual immorality by compromising the Word of God. They receive the teaching of Jezebel, which leads them into these grave sins. You can see it clearly in the Church. There are plenty of teachers and preachers ready to arm us with Scriptures that they twist into sanctions of sin.

I believe preachers take this route for one of two reasons: Either they are deceived, or they are trying to build a seeker-friendly congregation that is willing to sacrifice money in exchange for a message that excuses their sin. Either way, deception is in the mix because the latter group somehow has convinced themselves that teaching Christians to be successful and happy is more important than equipping them to grow up in Christ and effect positive change in the world around them.

We should not be surprised. Paul warned Timothy, "For the time will come when people will not put up with sound doctrine. . . . They will turn their ears away from the truth and turn aside to myths" (2 Timothy 4:3–4, NIV).

Let's look again at the myths that say it is okay to have sex before marriage. The root of this teaching is an encouragement to abuse sexual intimacy. Again, it is a subtle Jezebel deception. In order to unmask it, we have to get back to God's purpose for sex, and also understand that many people, even Christians, are searching for intimacy in all the wrong places and in many wrong ways. Keep this in mind: Any time we use something in a way for which it was not designed, we are abusing it. Damage is the likely result. (Think about the woman who breaks her high heel shoe by using it as a tool to hammer a nail into the wall.) Many good and godly things can be abused. Sex is part of God's design, but it is designed for married couples.

What is God's purpose for sex? Procreation (see Genesis 1:26–30) and to become one flesh (see Genesis 2:18–25). In short, God intended sex to be an intimate expression of love between husband and wife, an expression that bonds them together in unity. Make no mistake, God reserves sexual intimacy for marriage. C. S. Lewis puts it this way in his classic *Mere Christianity*:

> The Christian idea of marriage is based on Christ's words that a man and wife are to be regarded as a single organism. . . . [T]he male and female . . . were made to be combined together in pairs, not simply on a sexual level, but totally combined. The monstrosity of sexual intercourse outside marriage is that those who indulge in it are trying to isolate one kind of union (the sexual) from all the other kinds of union which were intended to go along with it and make up the total union. The Christian attitude does not

mean that there is anything wrong about sexual pleasure, any more than about the pleasure of eating. It means that you must not isolate that pleasure and try to get it by itself, any more than you ought to try to get the pleasures of taste without swallowing and digesting, by chewing things and spitting them out again.

As I mentioned earlier, Christian teaching abounds that sug- *Bulimia*
gests sex before marriage between two willing parties is not a sin. The reason given is that sexual intimacy is an expression of love. They contend that these partners are not violating—in fact, they are fulfilling—the one new commandment Jesus gave to "love one another" (John 13:34). Other teaching suggests that masturbation is acceptable for single Christians because it helps satisfy sexual appetites without fornicating. Others take the stance that whatever is not of faith is sin, so sexual encounters up to the point of fornication are a matter of conscience.

I am not here to draw lines around what you should or should not do in areas that are not clearly outlined in the Bible. The point is that the spirit of Jezebel will take a mile if you give it an inch. Once you start down the road to sexual arousal—either alone or with another (even another you love and plan to wed)—you can welcome spirits of lust or addiction that lead you down a darker path, one full of stumbling blocks.

Entire books have been written on this topic, so I will just reiterate the bottom line: God wants us to remain sexually pure until marriage. Immorality is abusing a gift of God by perverting its purpose. The God-ordained purpose of sexual intimacy is to make husband and wife one flesh (see Genesis 2:24). The sexual union is the means by which the two become one.

Jezebel Pushing *Porneia*

Jezebel does not have to entice you to commit fornication or adultery in order to lead you down the path to destruction.

John 13:34
Gen 2:24

Indeed, not all immoral relationships involve another party—at least not directly. Immorality is rushing into homes around the world through pornography, or porn. Noteworthy is the fact that the word *fornication* comes from the Greek world *porneia*, which means "illicit sexual intercourse." It is also a metaphor for the worship of idols. Once again, sexual immorality and idolatry meet up.

Consider some chilling statistics that demonstrate how the spirit of Jezebel has made inroads into our culture through porn. These figures are provided by pureHOPE (www.pure hope.net), an organization that offers Christian solutions in a sexualized culture. In the United States, Internet porn pulls in nearly $3 billion every year. The Internet porn industry worldwide is worth $5 billion. Some estimates for the entire "adult" industry—including Internet porn, video sales and rentals, cable television pay-per-view, phone sex, exotic dance clubs, magazines and novelty stories—are $13 billion a year. A disturbing number of Christians are sowing the money God gave them into this sordid industry.

If there could be one place protected from the deadly infection of pornography and sexual misconduct, one would assume that the Christian church would be that sanctuary. That was the reasoning at the onset of a study ChristiaNet (www.christianet .com) conducted in 2007. The results were startling: Church members, deacons, staff and even clergy are pursuing sexual gratification in ungodly ways. (See http://www.christianpost .com/news/porn-addiction-flooding-culture-church-27799/ for more information.)

The poll indicated that 50 percent of all Christian men and 20 percent of all Christian women in the United States are addicted to pornography. Yes, addicted. Not just one-time viewers or even frequent users. Addicted. What is more, 60 percent of the women who answered the survey admitted to having significant struggles with lust and 40 percent admitted to being involved in sexual sin in the past year. In a recent Pastors.com survey, 54 percent of pastors surveyed said they had viewed porn within the past year. Consider this: Even as the Church fights against the sex trade industry, part of the Church is unwittingly supporting it through pornography. The fight against this wickedness, then, is sadly ironic.

The prevalence of pornography also drives the temptation toward adultery. Research by sociologist Jill Manning indicates that pornography consumption is associated with several disturbing trends, including increased marital distress, risk of separation and divorce, infidelity and an increasing number of people struggling with compulsive and addictive sexual behavior. (See http://www.heritage.org/research/testimony/pornographys -impact-on-marriage-amp-the-family.)

The American Academy of Matrimonial Lawyers (www .aaml.org) reports that 68 percent of divorces involve one party meeting a new lover on the Internet, and 56 percent involve one party having an "obsessive interest in pornographic Web sites."

Although a 2009 Morality in Media (www.moralityinmedia .org) survey reports that 76 percent of adults in the United States agree that viewing hard-core adult pornography on the Internet is not morally acceptable, it is clear that moral boundaries are giving way to sexual immorality. Since Jesus said that every man who looks on a woman with lust for her has already committed adultery in his heart (see Matthew 5:27–28), we can conclude that Christians who view pornography are crossing the line of sexual immorality. Christians are serving the idol of pornography. And the spirit of Jezebel is pushing it. Remember, Jesus said that Jezebel teaches and seduces His servants to commit sexual immorality and eat things sacrificed to idols. Do not be fooled. Jezebel is a principality that is at work behind the scenes to push *porneia*.

Mat 5:27-28

Why Do We Tolerate Jezebel?

Jezebel is subtle. Just because a man is not watching pornography does not mean he is immune to sliding down Jezebel's slippery slope. Just because a woman is not having sex out of wedlock does not mean she is not tolerating the Jezebel spirit. Indeed, many pastors and believers who lead otherwise holy lives—and who are making positive impact in their communities—are nonetheless tolerating Jezebel. Remember the churches at Corinth and Thyatira.

Whenever we sit by and watch sin unfold without speaking the truth in love we are tolerating (and perhaps even endorsing by our silence) Jezebel's move in our midst. So why do we tolerate Jezebel? Beyond a lack of understanding about what Jezebel truly is, part of the problem is the "Hollywood Christianity Syndrome" that buys in to the hype without looking at character. But there is also lack of discernment in the Body of Christ that stems from believers relying on others to tell them what the Bible says instead of developing an intimate relationship with Christ themselves.

Jezebel is seducing believers and unbelievers alike with false doctrine and false anointing. But that does not have to happen. Jesus has given each of us individual responsibility to be students of the Word and to avoid deception. The New Testament is full of warnings not to be deceived. This means we cannot blame our pastor or our best friend or our television or our computer if we fall into Jezebel's trap. Until we understand the potential for deception that every one of us faces in a world saturated with immorality and idolatry, we run a great risk of being on the wrong side in the end time Church.

Eph 4: 11-13

Matt 1:19

Romans 5:20 ; 6: 1-2

Ps 97: 10

Prov. 7: 21-23

1 Sam 13-14

Duet 17½ - 14:20

I Kings 10:26, 28-29 ; 10: 14 - 23

I Kings 11: 1- 3

3

The Depths of Satan

There is something of an anomaly in the life of the Church today. On the one hand, many churches—and the American Church predominates in this—have been accused of shallow Christianity. Some of the sermons broadcasted over the airwaves sound more like motivational seminars than the pick-up-your-cross-and-follow-Christ messages the apostles taught in the early days of the Church. Pastors are turning a blind eye to sin for the sake of church growth while others are themselves engaging in behind-the-scenes abominations.

On the other hand, vast multitudes of hungry, sold-out, on-fire believers are seeking the deep things of God. In a movement growing all over the world, the Church is a place where you can be rooted and grounded in love, able to comprehend the width, length, depth and height of the love of Christ, which surpasses knowledge, so that you can be filled with all the fullness of God (see Ephesians 3:17–19). It is a place of intimacy with the Father, Son and Holy Ghost that marks believers who seek first

Eph 3:17-19

the Kingdom of God with zeal for the cause of Christ. It is a breath of fresh Holy Spirit air.

Hungry believers are desperately seeking the deep things of God, the hidden wisdom that God ordained before the ages for our glory (see 1 Corinthians 2:7). The Bible promises us over and over again that our loving God is waiting and welcoming us into a deeper, more intimate relationship with Him. When we search for God with our whole heart, we will find Him (see Jeremiah 29:13). We are assured that when we come near to God He will come near to us (see James 4:8). We know that the Holy Spirit searches all things, yes, even the deep things of God (see 1 Corinthians 2:10).

And yet, as hard as it may be to believe, the peril that so easily overtakes the "shallow" churches also creeps in among the burning and shining ones who love God with all their mind, all their heart, soul and strength. That peril is called Jezebel.

Gold Dust and Gemstones

Jezebel's deception is increasing in the Western Church. Perhaps you are aware of the controversy around issues like the sudden appearance of gold dust and small gemstones during worship services, as well as encounters with female angels usually welcomed by New Age mystics.

Deception can also creep in when immature believers seek attention by giving false impressions of Holy Ghost manifestations—like uncontrollable screaming in the middle of worship, writhing on the ground like a snake, pretending to smoke invisible marijuana cigarettes to get high on Jesus and meowing like cats during sermons.

Any uncontrolled and disruptive behavior, left uncorrected, can lead to a culture of manifestations that set the stage for the Jezebel deception. Please understand that I am not talking about

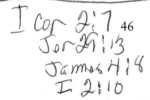

46

genuine experiences like being slain in the Spirit or shaking in His presence. I am talking about demonic manifestations that people pass off as the Holy Spirit in the name of Jesus.

It is true that our God is a supernatural God. He loves us and He wants us to seek His face. It is also true that when He arrives on the scene supernatural things can—and often do—manifest. He loves to heal and to deliver. But at the same time, wicked spirits lie in wait to deceive the sincere believer who has, in his zeal, started seeking encounters in the spiritual realm instead of seeking the God of the spiritual realm. The desire for supernatural encounters can lead us smack-dab into the middle of the depths of Satan, a place where the spirit of Jezebel dwells.

Satanical Delusions and Devices

It seems ironic on the surface that Jezebel dwelled in the church at Thyatira, a church that was growing in good works. As we noted earlier, the Son of God pointed specifically to the love, service, faith and patience in this community of believers (see Revelation 2:19). This local church was zealous for the cause of Christ. One could describe many—and probably most—of its members as loving servant-leaders who exercised faith to win souls for Jesus.

Let that be a lesson for us about looking at surface fruit only. Just because a church is growing—or holds mega-church status—does not mean that sin is not abounding there or that Jezebel is not seducing the saints. Too many believers let their guard down because of impressive religious presentations. Many of us have been in churches where the outside of the cup is clean but inside it is full of extortion and excess (see Matthew 23:25). The congregation cannot see anything but the bright and shining display, and so continues feeding the system that

Rev 2:19
Matt 23:25

Jezebel corrupted long before. The thing is, of course, they are not fooling Jesus.

Jesus had reasons to rejoice over the Thyatiran church and was quick to commend the congregation. He was deeply grieved, however, because some of the very souls that were translated out of the kingdom of darkness and into His Kingdom of light would experience only short-lived freedom. He warned that some of those souls had been and would be wooed into the depths of Satan by "that woman Jezebel, who calls herself a prophetess, to teach and seduce [My] servants to commit sexual immorality and eat things sacrificed to idols" (Revelation 2:20). I surmise, by the way, that the woman took on that name as part of her bravado.

It was not merely the influence of a controlling, strong-willed woman in the Thyatiran church that troubled Jesus so. It was not teaching from a sincere believer who had misinterpreted Scripture that gave Jesus concern. No, Jesus described the doctrine that was being promoted as "the depths of Satan" (Revelation 2:24). That is serious. What are the depths of Satan? Matthew Henry's *Commentary* calls the depths of Satan "Satanical delusions and devices, diabolical mysteries."

Essentially, the depths of Satan are doctrines that persuade people to believe that they alone have deep insight into religion—even when it opposes the Scriptures. Jezebel was teaching fellow members of the church at Thyatira to commit sexual immorality and eat things sacrificed to idols. With this teaching, she was directly opposing the wisdom of the apostolic fathers—and succeeding.

In those early days of the growing Church, a conflict had developed over whether or not Gentiles should be circumcised according to the custom of Moses in order to be saved. The apostles and elders came together to consider the matter—the meeting of the Jerusalem Council described in Acts 15. There

Rev 2:20, 24

was great dispute, but ultimately the council agreed with James that "we should not trouble those from among the Gentiles who are turning to God, but that we write to them to abstain from things polluted by idols, from sexual immorality, from things strangled, and from blood" (Acts 15:19–20).

By promoting idolatry and sexual immorality, Jezebel was teaching the very opposite of Holy Ghost–inspired wisdom. In doing so, she was leading Thyatiran believers out of the will of God and into the depths of Satan, who comes to steal, kill and destroy.

The spirit of Jezebel will be punished for leading believers into the depths of Satan, but that does not let believers off the hook. Because Jesus loves us so, those who allow false doctrines to lead them off the narrow path will also meet with suffering if they do not repent (see Revelation 2:22), and those who teach others what Jezebel has taught them will be struck dead (see Revelation 2:23). It is a sobering truth. But these pronouncements come from the love of God in an effort to wake up those who have fallen into the trap of this powerful spirit so they can escape.

Doctrines of Demons 3/2 8

Although we understand from Scripture that many who depart from the faith in the end times will become propagators of "doctrines of demons" (see 1 Timothy 4:1), we learn from these words of Jesus in Revelation that false doctrines also circulate freely among the Body of Christ. Remember, "evil men and imposters will grow worse and worse, deceiving and being deceived" (2 Timothy 3:13).

Doctrines of demons oppose biblical principles. One popular example in recent years comes from high-profile preachers who claim there is no hell. Jesus confirms the concepts of hell, eternal fire, outer darkness and eternal punishment in more

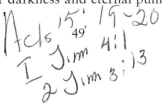

Acts 15: 19~20
49
I Jim 4:1
2 Jim 3:13

than 45 New Testament verses. In another example, the Bible talks of an errant teaching that forbids marriage—a doctrine of demons that opens the door to sexual perversion and abuse (see 1 Timothy 4:3). Angel worship is a doctrine of demons. Legalism is also a doctrine of demons—and the driving force behind the murderous religious spirit.

I believe that many false doctrines in the Christian Church stem from a lack of balance between understanding the love of God and having a healthy, reverential fear of the Lord. That lack of balance opens the door to seducing spirits like Jezebel. Some believers receive this unbalanced teaching—which often fails to discuss the true meaning of repentance—as a license to crawl back up into Big Daddy's lap for consolation and another blessing when they have finished sinning.

Jezebel's doctrine of demons perverts the grace of God and, in doing so, ultimately seduces believers into a lifestyle of immorality and idol worship. These individuals request God's forgiveness, but give no indication of true repentance. Yes, the Father loves us unconditionally, but that does not give us a license to practice sin. Jezebel's false teachings convince believers they are in right standing with God because of the grace of God, even though they keep practicing the same sin without any godly sorrow or real desire to change.

God is long-suffering and He will forgive us. But we must confess our sins in order to receive forgiveness and cleansing from our faithful, just and loving God (see 1 John 1:9). We must turn from our wicked ways, relying on the grace of God to help us as we wage war against sin. We have to truly repent.

Perverting God's Grace

It is not possible to be intimate with Christ and intimate with sin at the same time. Paul put it this way, "Shall we continue in

sin that grace may abound? Certainly not! How shall we who died to sin live any longer in it?" (Romans 6:1–2).

Sound doctrine teaches believers who they are in Christ—no longer slaves to sin, but saints who can resist the devil by co-operating with the grace of God. The Bible is clear that false teachers will abound in the last days—and that

> the time will come when [Christians] will not endure sound doctrine, but according to their own desires, because they have itching ears, they will heap up for themselves [false] teachers; and they will turn their ears away from the truth, and be turned aside to fables.
>
> 2 Timothy 4:3–4

Jezebel's false teaching on the grace of God is a doctrine of demons, the depths of Satan. Peter warned that false prophets—and we can include false prophetesses—would arise, along with false teachers, who secretly introduce destructive heresies, "even denying the Lord who bought them" (2 Peter 2:1). Paul warned of those who distort the Gospel of Christ (see Galatians 1:7).

Please do not misunderstand me. God is full of grace and mercy. We know the grace of God that brings salvation has appeared to all men. But Paul taught his spiritual son Titus that "denying ungodliness and worldly lusts, we should live soberly, righteously, and godly in the present age" (Titus 2:11–13).

God's grace empowers us to live according to His Word. Doctrines of demons, however, soothe itching ears listening for the go-ahead to sin without forfeiting intimacy with the Father, Son and Holy Spirit. As Jude puts it, those teachers come from "certain men [who] have crept in unnoticed, who long ago were marked out for this condemnation, ungodly men, who turn the grace of our God into lewdness and deny the only Lord God and our Lord Jesus Christ" (Jude 4). Again, one of those teachers is Jezebel.

2 Peter 2:1
Gal 1:7
Titus 2:11–13
Jude 4

51

Jezebel's Gospel Distortions

I lived for thirteen months in a tiny town in America's deep South—a wilderness time in which God was separating me from negative influences and preparing me to walk in His calling. In my search for a home church, I had the opportunity to explore many different denominations. The differences in doctrine amazed me at times. Some churches, for instance, did not condone live music. Others did not allow women to preach.

But it was the extremes of teaching on God's grace that really shocked me. Those extremes ranged from über holiness that left no room for second chances to turning a blind eye to sin so long as you kept the Gospel buzzwords handy.

I will never forget standing on my Alabama porch with some of my neighbors one evening. One of the young men, Mike, was recently married. His father-in-law was the pastor of a denominational church that he was trying to convince me to visit. I was all ears, but what I heard convinced me I needed to run in the other direction—and fast. It was Mike's perversion of God's grace that was so troubling.

Mike openly discussed his drinking habit and his tendency to have sex with other women while on his binges. He quickly assured me that "it's under the blood" despite not showing any sign of true remorse. I cannot judge his heart, but the confession of his mouth told me that he had not fallen into sin and repented. He was practicing sin, and assuring himself that anything he did was cleansed by virtue of his being "under the blood." I felt sure that his father-in-law pastor and his newlywed wife had no idea that he was essentially a cheating drunk who eased his conscience with the soothing sounds of false doctrine.

Teaching that Papa God pardons sin before we repent is distorting the Gospel of Christ.

If we [freely] admit that we have sinned and confess our sins, He is faithful and just (true to His own nature and promises) and will forgive our sins [dismiss our lawlessness] and [continuously] cleanse us from all unrighteousness [everything not in conformity to His will in purpose, thought, and action].

1 John 1:9, AMPLIFIED

The key words in this amplified Scripture are *freely admit that we have sinned*. God will forgive us of anything—no matter how horrific—if we admit that we have sinned, confess our sins and ask for forgiveness. If we do not freely admit we have sinned and confess our sins, we are only fooling ourselves, and our intimate fellowship with the Father remains broken.

God, in His kindness and mercy, has patience with compromising believers. Jesus even gave "that woman Jezebel" space to repent (see Revelation 2:21). But God does not forgive those who refuse to repent, even if they are in full-time ministry, prophesying, casting out devils and doing signs and wonders in the name of Jesus (see Matthew 7:22).

When we come boldly to His throne to obtain mercy and find grace to help in time of need, it implies coming to a seat of authority with fear of the Lord (see Hebrews 4:14–16). We want to trade what we deserve (judgment for our sins) for what we do not deserve (grace to purify our hearts and strengthen us not to continue practicing sin). After all, Jesus' grace is sufficient for us and His strength is made perfect in weakness (see 2 Corinthians 12:9). But we have to repent. We have to be willing to declare war on that sin and keep battling against it until we get the victory.

Yes, it is true that where sin abounds, grace abounds much more (see Romans 5:20). It is true that we are not under law but under grace. But that does not mean that we should make ourselves slaves to sin, which leads to death (see Romans 6:15–16). When we sin, God does not want us to punish ourselves or

Rev 2:21
53
matt 7:22

wallow in condemnation for a month. He does want us to turn to Him with all of our hearts, with fasting, with weeping and with mourning over our rebellion (see Joel 2:12).

Jezebel's gospel defies genuine repentance and shuts out the Spirit of grace with a stance of pride that comes before the public fall. God resists the proud (see James 4:6).

Jezebel's Untouchables

Some churches have member hierarchies based on bloodlines, financial giving, talent or the fact that they have been in the church since the first day it opened. To ordain ministers and choose department leaders based on anything beyond prophetic wisdom is like a welcome mat for the enemy. Over and again in Scripture we see the Holy Ghost separating out missionaries (see Acts 13:2), and there are direct guidelines for appointing deacons (see 1 Timothy 3:12). The point is this: All promotion should come from God not from man.

Some pastors appoint their sons and daughters as youth leaders despite the notable absence of any discernible call. Some apostles designate prophets based solely on decades of loyalty to the ministry, despite little sign of Christ's character in them. Although spiritual leaders may feel legitimate pressure to build a staff with whomever they can trust, filling these offices by bloodlines, financial giving, talent or loyalty indicates nepotism (special favor based on family ties) and cronyism (appointing longtime friends to positions based on relationship rather than calling).

Certainly not all churches and ministries that are "family-run"—meaning that the pastor's family and close friends hold positions of responsibility—are in error. The positioning may simply be an expedient way to fill roles in a new or growing congregation. But there are many cases of churches and ministries in which nepotism and cronyism are the means to keep control tightly in the hands of the senior pastor and his or her chosen ones. These individuals act essentially like Jezebel's eunuchs.

The Bible teaches against favoritism (see James 2:1). Although nepotism and cronyism can happen innocently, it can nevertheless set the stage for what I call "Jezebel's untouchables." An inner circle forms and holds tightly the reins of all that happens within the four walls of the church—and sometimes beyond—lording authority over the sheep. Where nepotism and cronyism are present, the inner circle often subscribes to extreme loyalty to the senior pastor, even at the risk of disloyalty to the purposes of God and abuse of the sheep. This inner circle of untouchables may even verbalize covenants of loyalty to the group. Anyone who breaks the covenant—man or woman—is persecuted and labeled (ironically) with a rebellious, prideful Jezebel spirit.

These untouchables are warned against ever leaving the inner circle. Sometimes they are cursed with the assurance that they will lose their anointing and miss their destiny if they break free. These are signs of a church where Jezebel has taken over the leadership.

Here is what this looks like in the everyday operations of the local church. Let's say that a parent is concerned about something inappropriate that happened to a child in the nursery. The senior pastor does not investigate the problem. In fact, he dismisses the complaint because his daughter is the head of the department—and more children suffer. Or say that a member of the presbytery is offering unwelcomed flirtation to one of the church volunteers, and she confronts him. That presbyter labels the woman a troublemaker, even a Jezebel, and she is made to feel so unwelcome and uncomfortable that she eventually leaves. If a woman with a strong personality has ideas about how to improve the flow of Sunday school children back into the sanctuary and asks to speak to the pastor about it, the administrator feels threatened and labels her a Jezebel. The staff is warned that this Jezebel is looking for a way to get close to the pastor. She is shunned and her valuable insights are ignored.

At times, it seems as though people operating in a spirit of Jezebel are staying one step ahead of the game, falsely "discerning" and wrongly accusing others of flowing in this spirit, without understanding the accusations they are making.

An Untouchable's Demise

Oftentimes these untouchables are celebrated publicly, but they may be abused or neglected privately. In other words, these eunuchs are not getting their spiritual needs met. They are too busy serving the pastor's vision to get the help they need for themselves and their families. They are encouraged, instead, to stay busy working in the church to avoid the temptations of the devil.

This was the case of a young man who served as a maintenance worker in a particular church. "Rick" was struggling with an addiction to crack cocaine. This addiction lasted for years, and everyone in the church knew it, including the pastoral staff. Rather than mandating counseling for the young man, however, the staff ignored the addiction in favor of his faithful church service, even if he came to church high. His work for the church seemed to be all that mattered.

Despite knowledge of his idolatry (drugs were his idol), the pastoral staff endorsed his marriage to a young woman who worked in the children's ministry. The couple soon had a baby, but even with the many changes in his life, Rick never overcame his drug addiction. He would often receive public deliverance ministry and prophetic words about a new beginning from the staff, but he would quickly relapse. Rather than offer substantial help to Rick, the church leadership continued cleaning up the fruit of his addiction and allowing him to continue in his idolatrous state, even as it slowly destroyed his life and family. As long as he showed up to serve on time, he was untouchable.

Sometimes during church services, Rick would steal money from purses left in the seats by women who went up to the altar for prayer. Once, a member of the church called the police after $500 was missing from her purse. Rick was the only one in the room who was not at the altar at the time the money was taken. He was sitting in the last row after having just received deliverance ministry for his addiction—again.

The pastoral staff, however, did not investigate the member's claim that Rick stole the money. The message was clear: It would have damaged their credibility as deliverance ministers. After all, Rick had "just been delivered" that very night from drug addiction. If Rick stole the money, it would embarrass the senior pastor. The pastoral staff rebuked the woman for calling the police, and suggested she repent or leave the church. The church's doctrine regarding Rick—"We have cast the devil out of him, so he doesn't need professional help"—was out of balance. They chose to ignore the fact that he was not getting better.

Some years later, Rick was caught robbing a convenience store to support his drug habit. His wife left him in despair because she could no longer deal with his addiction.

Rick is in prison and his daughter is now without a father because an authoritarian church with a false doctrine about deliverance failed to show him the true love of God. The selfish desire for Rick's work at the church plus pride in its deliverance ministry let him fall into the depths of Satan. Rick was allowed to pervert the grace of God for a season, but his sin eventually found him out.

Another victim of Jezebel.

4

Riding the Back of Babylon

The spirit of Jezebel, which is often camouflaged, has a partner that stays equally well hidden.

The prophet Isaiah quotes the boasting of this fellow spirit: The Lady of the Kingdoms brags, "No one sees me" (Isaiah 47:10). The Lady of the Kingdoms is Babylon, religious running mate of Jezebel. Part of Jezebel's end time purpose is to seduce people to worship the Lady of the Kingdoms instead of the King of kings. It may begin with control and manipulation but the motive is murder.

The Lady of the Kingdoms is known in the book of Revelation as "Mystery, Babylon the Great, the Mother of Harlots and of the abominations of the earth" (Revelation 17:5). Jezebel and her behind-the-scenes counterpart—Mystery Babylon, the Lady of the Kingdoms, the Mother of Harlots—have seduced countless numbers into sexual immorality and idolatry.

Furthermore, Jezebel and Babylon drive the spirit of the world to accomplish their goals. In this chapter we will define and study the motivation and interaction of these powerful spirits, and see how they are setting up their seductions for end time destruction.

Beware the Spirit of the World

Let's begin with a definition of the spirit of the world. Together, Jezebel and Babylon help the spirit of the world execute its deadly agenda. The spirit of the world is the spirit that murdered Jesus, His apostles, Paul—and it moves strongly against anyone who names the name of Christ.

To be sure, all believers are in a war that will determine their allegiance: Christ or the world. Will we obey the lust of the eyes, the lust of the flesh and the pride of life? Or will we obey the Word of God and the Spirit of God?

Scripture gives us this warning:

Do not love the world or the things in the world. If anyone loves the world, the love of the Father is not in him. For all that is in the world—the lust of the flesh, the lust of the eyes, and the pride of life—is not of the Father but is of the world. And the world is passing away, and the lust of it; but he who does the will of God abides forever.

1 John 2:15–17

John was talking about the spirit of the world, not the world itself. We know that

"God so loved the world that He gave His only begotten Son, that whoever believes in Him should not perish but have everlasting life. For God did not send His Son into the world to condemn the world, but that the world through Him might be saved."

John 3:16–17

But loving the spirit of the world is another matter entirely.

Careful Scripture studies reveal that Jesus and His disciples battled against the spirit of the world, which battled against them. The New Testament warns repeatedly against embracing this spirit. James compelled us to keep ourselves unstained by the world (see James 1:27), and that a friend of the world makes himself an enemy of God (James 4:4). Paul said not to be "conformed to this world" (Romans 12:2). John told us: "Do not love the world or the things in the world. If anyone loves the world, the love of the Father is not in him" (1 John 2:15).

The Great Falling Away

Scripture reveals that these spirits are in operation right before the return of the Lord. Indeed, they play a role in the great falling away from the faith at the end of the age, of which Paul warned us. Paul was moving in a prophetic anointing when he penned his epistles, which often warn of deception. In particular, there are two instances in which Paul spoke of this falling away: 1 Timothy 4:1–3 and 2 Thessalonians 2:1–4.

Here is the first:

> Now the Spirit expressly says that in latter times some will depart from the faith, giving heed to deceiving spirits and doctrines of demons, speaking lies in hypocrisy, having their own conscience seared with a hot iron, forbidding to marry, and commanding to abstain from foods which God created to be received with thanksgiving by those who believe and know the truth.
>
> 1 Timothy 4:1–3

Jezebel and Babylon are both among the deceiving spirits that spew forth the doctrines of demons. Paul outlined a couple of the doctrines of demons in this verse, but these are by far not the only doctrines that the spirit of this world is peddling. Doctrines of demons have made their way into our schools, into our churches and into our media.

Look again at these words of Paul:

> The time will come when they will not endure sound doctrine, but according to their own desires, because they have itching ears, they will heap up for themselves teachers; and they will turn their ears away from the truth, and be turned aside to fables.
>
> 2 Timothy 4:3–4

I bear witness that we are in this time now. Much of the Church has itching ears for a prosperity gospel or other "feel-good" gospels that cater to the desires of our flesh, and therein dull our spirits to the truth Jesus preached.

This watered-down gospel is opening the door to the great falling away. James said that if we are hearers of the Word only—if we do not obey the Word we hear—we are deceiving ourselves (see James 1:22). It is not too hard for Jezebel and Babylon to deceive us when we have already deceived ourselves with a gospel that demands no endurance to walk out.

When the Lord returns, He must find us faithful to His Word. He who endures to the end will be saved (see Matthew 24:13). That does not mean we are perfect, but it does mean we engage actively in the war against the spirit of the world. It is tragic that many will fall away from the faith before the Second Coming of our Lord Jesus Christ.

Here is the second specific verse warning of a falling away:

> Now, brethren, concerning the coming of our Lord Jesus Christ and our gathering together to Him, we ask you, not to be soon shaken in mind or troubled, either by spirit or by word or by letter, as if from us, as though the day of Christ had come. Let no one deceive you by any means; for that Day will not come unless the falling away comes first, and the man of sin is revealed, the son of perdition, who opposes and exalts himself above all that is called God or that is worshiped, so that he sits as God in the temple of God, showing himself that he is God.
>
> 2 Thessalonians 2:1–4

This falling away from the faith—this turning away from Christ—will be so clear that it is marked as one of the signs preceding the Second Coming, along with the appearance of the Antichrist. I believe this great falling away begins with the Church's compromise with the spirit of the world—which is already rampant in Western churches. Babylon and Jezebel are co-laboring to seduce the saints with immorality and idolatry that will mark them for the lake of fire when Jesus returns, if they do not repent. The spirit of the world is like a tool in their hands.

Babylon: The World's System

There are conflicting views in the Body of Christ regarding where Babylon falls in the demonic hierarchy (principality, power, ruler of darkness, etc.). What is clear, however, is that Babylon is more than a seducing spirit: It manifests in the world as a system.

Babylon is the worldwide religious, political and economic system personified in the book of Revelation as *Mystery Babylon*. I believe that Jezebel is a principality and Mystery Babylon is the world's system through which it works. Some consider Babylon to be the emerging One World Government or New World Order. Strong's concordance defines *Mystery Babylon* as "the secret of confusion or bitterness." The most important thing to understand is that the spirit behind this system is powerful and deadly.

In Revelation 17:1–6, John offers a glimpse into the spirit of Babylon:

> Then one of the seven angels who had the seven bowls came and talked with me, saying to me, "Come, I will show you the judgment of the great harlot who sits on many waters, with whom the kings of the earth committed fornication, and the inhabitants of the earth were made drunk with the wine of her fornication."

63

So he carried me away in the Spirit into the wilderness. And I saw a woman sitting on a scarlet beast which was full of names of blasphemy, having seven heads and ten horns. The woman was arrayed in purple and scarlet, and adorned with gold and precious stones and pearls, having in her hand a golden cup full of abominations and the filthiness of her fornication. And on her forehead a name was written:

MYSTERY, BABYLON THE GREAT,
THE MOTHER OF HARLOTS AND OF
THE ABOMINATIONS OF THE EARTH.

I saw the woman, drunk with the blood of the saints and with the blood of the martyrs of Jesus. And when I saw her, I marveled with great amazement.

This great harlot seduces the world's leaders—the religious, political and economic leaders—working like a hidden puppet master pulling the strings. Babylon's system woos people with its many benefits, such as a one-world religion that promises fewer wars (and rumors of wars) and prosperity. We see this edging into the Body of Christ today through universalism, New Age doctrine, humanism and a prosperity gospel. Babylon is full of idolatry and immorality because its systems were birthed through Jezebel.

Infiltrating the World's Systems

The angel who spoke with John in the passage above essentially offered him prophetic insight into one of Satan's maneuvers to seduce not only the Church, but also the nation of Israel and the world. By infiltrating the political, economic and religious systems, Babylon will gain a stronghold.

Regarding politics, Revelation 18:3 reveals that "all the nations have drunk of the wine of the wrath of her fornication, the kings of the earth have committed fornication with her." In this verse we can clearly see Babylon's influence on world government.

Regarding economics, Revelation 18:3 says this about the marketplace: "The merchants of the earth have become rich through the abundance of her luxury." Revelation 18:23 states: "For your merchants were the great men of the earth, for by your sorcery all the nations were deceived." Many financially influential figures of the end times will be in bondage to Babylon and not see it.

Regarding religion, Revelation 17:5, as we have seen, calls her "the Mother of Harlots." Some theologians consider this name to be symbolic of various apostate religions that will be linked together and dominate the world until the Antichrist comes to full power. They suggest that this great whore will hold power over her loyal subjects by her spiritual harlotry and abominations.

For most believers, this is all a mystery. The important thing is that we begin to understand how Jezebel and Babylon work together so that we can discern the subtle temptation to compromise. We can do that by searching Scripture, of course, but we also can gain some insight by observing the history of these spirits in ancient times. Let's take a few moments to see the early appearance of the spirit of Babylon in our world, particularly as it has partnered with Jezebel.

Nimrod's New Religion

Jezebel and Babylon have a long history with one another. Many who teach about the Jezebel spirit first identify it plainly in the Old Testament queen for whom it is named. But the spirit that influenced Queen Jezebel was alive and well long before she personified many of its traits. Much the same, Mystery Babylon has been around for ages.

Some believe the spirit of Babylon was at work in the Garden of Eden, moving through the serpent to convince Eve to seek forbidden knowledge. And Scripture offers a hint into this spirit's motives to build an economic system apart from the Kingdom of God in Genesis 10:8–12, which is where Nimrod, great-grandson of Noah, enters the scene. Nimrod founded various cities in the land of Shinar, including Babel (an early name for the city of Babylon) and established a kingdom. This realm also was called Babylon.

Bible historians note that Nimrod led the Tower of Babel project as an act of rebellion. In fact, we get a clue into Nimrod's character by his name: The Hebrew word *nimrod* means "let us rebel." First-century Jewish historian Flavius Josephus made this comment: "[Nimrod] said he would be revenged on God, if he should have a mind to drown the world again; for that he would build a tower too high for the waters to be able to reach!" What arrogance! It was as if Nimrod was saying, "We'll show God! We'll do what we want and He can't judge us!"

Nimrod married a pagan woman named Semiramis. That is where Nimrod's Babylonian story takes a Jezebelic twist. Semiramis was also known as Ishtar or the Queen of Heaven. Semiramis has many of the same characteristics as Queen Jezebel. She is the one who introduced sexual immorality into pagan religion. In fact, like Semiramis, Jezebel is also known as Ishtar or the Queen of Heaven. Semiramis exhibited the first recorded manifestation of what we call Jezebel.

Semiramis's Idolatry

Semiramis, who had boasted of being a virgin queen, became pregnant after Nimrod's death. By coming up with a clever story, she found a way both to cover her immorality and to deify her late husband: She declared that the spirit of Nimrod had gotten her pregnant.

Semiramis's son, who was named Tammuz, was introduced as a reincarnated Nimrod and positioned as a god. Semiramis soon became the mother of a cult that claimed divine wisdom, but, like the Jezebel of the book of Revelation, she taught her followers to serve idols and to commit sexual immorality. Semiramis promoted a perverted trinity—herself, the dead Nimrod and Tammuz—and introduced fertility cults.

We see evidence of this in Scripture: The Lord showed Ezekiel women sitting at the north gate of His house weeping for Tammuz (see Ezekiel 8:14). The *Reformation Study Bible* gives this description:

> At the time of Ezekiel, Tammuz was worshiped both as a fertility god and the lord of the underworld. Rites used in worship of Tammuz were tied to the annual cycles of death and rebirth of vegetation. When plants withered under the heat of the summer sun, Tammuz was thought to have died and descended to the underworld; mourning rites marked his passing. The reappearance of vegetation was viewed as the return of Tammuz; fertility rites sought to ensure the productivity of the land.

In *Meditations in the Revelation* (Zion Faith Homes, 1991), Rex Andrews explains that Babylonian girls were steeped in fertility cult rites and offered the most precious gifts they could devote: their virginity, chastity and modesty. Rather than bowing to the one true God, Andrews reports that every knee bowed to the goddess, every hand was stretched out to her, every lip revered her name. That name was Ishtar, an alias for Semiramis and also Jezebel.

Andrews states:

> One of the hallowed fundamentals of the worship of Ishtar obliged every woman who believed in her and worshiped in her

Temple to give herself at least once in her life to a strange man. This obligation was universal without respect to age or rank. Every female worshipper had to sit in the sanctuary with veiled face and expose her nakedness to the lustful eyes of strange males. If a man halted in front of a woman and desired to have intercourse with her, he would, as a sign of his desire, place a piece of silver or some article of value in her bosom. The woman was then compelled to surrender to his lust. The priests took this gift as an offering for the goddess Ishtar.

Besides this compulsory whoredom which was carried on by the priests of Ishtar, there were attached to the Temple permanent harlot votaries, or *kedeshot* (viz: holy, sanctified to Ishtar for harlotry). During the spring festival, when Ishtar descended into Sheol (made into a theatrical) to beg the shades to release Tammuz from the bonds of deathly slumber and send him back to earth to renew its fruitfulness and fertility, the *kedeshot* participated in the wildest orgies in the Temple in honor of returning newborn Tammuz.

The Jezebel-Babylon Connection

Are you beginning to see the strength of the Jezebel-Babylon connection? Although the Bible does not mention Semiramis by name, Bible historians largely credit her with developing the system of pagan worship in Babylon.

The spirit of Jezebel—the spirit that influenced Semiramis—is ultimately the founder of the Babylonian religious system. Although Nimrod founded the city of Babylon, Semiramis in her quest for power created its religion. Babylon's religion is Jezebel's religion. The Old Testament's Queen Jezebel followed those same pagan practices and rituals.

The point is this: Jezebel is a spiritual harlot and so is Mystery Babylon. Consider the Scriptures. Every single one of the ninety Old Testament references to Israel's harlotry speaks of a religion that seeks to have its needs met through idolatry. Babylon is called the Mother of Harlots, which means she births other religions. Almost every false religion in the world today is tied in some way to the cult Semiramis founded. The Revelation 2:20 Jezebel was teaching God's servants the ways of Babylon.

Regarding Israel, the Lord told Ezekiel that He was "crushed by their adulterous heart which has departed from Me, and by their eyes which play the harlot after their idols; they will loathe themselves for the evils which they committed in all their abominations" (Ezekiel 6:9). Israel repeatedly put its trust in idols, hoping to receive provision, and forged alliances with other idolatrous nations in exchange for protection. This hurt the heart of God. Israel was supposed to stand for God, not compromise with the spirit of Babylon.

While they were in the wilderness, the Lord told the Israelites:

> "Take heed to yourself, lest you make a covenant with the inhabitants of the land where you are going, lest it be a snare in your midst. But you shall destroy their altars, break their sacred pillars, and cut down their wooden images (for you shall worship no other god, for the LORD, whose name is Jealous, is a jealous God), lest you make a covenant with the inhabitants of the land, and they play the harlot with their gods and make sacrifice to their gods, and one of them invites you and you eat of his sacrifice, and you take of his daughters for your sons, and his daughters play the harlot with their gods and make your sons play the harlot with their gods."
>
> Exodus 34:12–16

Think about it for a minute. Israel had a covenant with God. Only one party in a covenant could be considered a harlot, because a harlot by definition is one who is unfaithful. Mystery Babylon is called the Mother of Harlots, indicating that this is a powerful spirit that seduces others into spiritual harlotry.

Another way to describe spiritual harlotry is idolatry. Idolatry is worshiping another god—and idolatry tends to lead to immorality of all sorts, from sexual sins to drugs to human trafficking to various demon-inspired rituals. This is Jezebel's domain. Jezebel uses Babylon to forward its wicked agenda.

Finally She Falls

Jezebel is indeed on a quest for power and control—and it wants the whole world to worship its gods. This spirit wants everyone to worship the harlot Babylon, which is a counterfeit of the Bride of Christ. Mystery Babylon and Jezebel are working together to deceive the Church. At the end of the age, the Bride of Christ will engage in spiritual conflict with Mystery Babylon.

There are many theories about Babylon and how it manifests in the last days. I will leave those discussions to the theologians who have dedicated many years of study to the topic. What is important for our study of Jezebel is the fact that Babylon falls just as Isaiah prophesied (see Isaiah 21:9). Two verses in Revelation declare a fall of Babylon: Revelation 14:8 and 18:2. This suggests either that there are two stages to the fall of this wicked system, or that it falls twice.

Revelation 14:8 tells why Babylon falls: "Babylon is fallen, is fallen, that great city, because she has made all nations drink of the wine of the wrath of her fornication." Revelation 18:2–10 shows us the result of the fall, reminds us why it fell and calls the saints out of Babylon. In this second passage we see God's judgment on Babylon and all those who refuse to turn their backs on this demon-inspired system:

> "Babylon the great is fallen, is fallen, and has become a dwelling place of demons, a prison for every foul spirit, and a cage for every unclean and hated bird! For all the nations have drunk of the wine of the wrath of her fornication, the kings of the earth

have committed fornication with her, and the merchants of the earth have become rich through the abundance of her luxury."

And I heard another voice from heaven saying, "Come out of her, my people, lest you share in her sins, and lest you receive of her plagues. For her sins have reached to heaven, and God has remembered her iniquities. Render to her just as she rendered to you, and repay her double according to her works; in the cup which she has mixed, mix double for her. In the measure that she glorified herself and lived luxuriously, in the same measure give her torment and sorrow; for she says in her heart, 'I sit as queen, and am no widow, and will not see sorrow.' Therefore her plagues will come in one day—death and mourning and famine. And she will be utterly burned with fire, for strong is the Lord God who judges her.

"The kings of the earth who committed fornication and lived luxuriously with her will weep and lament for her, when they see the smoke of her burning, standing at a distance for fear of her torment, saying, 'Alas, alas, that great city Babylon, that mighty city! For in one hour your judgment has come.'"

Jezebel's counterfeit religious system, the mighty Babylon, which has held believers and unbelievers captive for thousands of years, will be destroyed in a single hour.

5

Jezebel's Religion

Are you religious? If you are a sincere believer in Jesus and familiar with His words to the spiritual leaders of His day, you probably cringe if someone hints that you might be "religious." Religious spirits spark debates that breed strife among Christians (see 2 Timothy 2:14). They also prevent people from entering the Kingdom of God (see Matthew 23:13).

For most Christians, the words *religious* and *religious spirit* bring to mind images of the Pharisees and Sadducees—the religious officials who refused to believe that Jesus was the Son of God and demanded His crucifixion. So if someone suggests you are religious, you are probably quick to explain that you are in relationship with Jesus. You don't have a religious bone in your body—nor does your Savior.

But with whom do you have a relationship, really? Hold that thought.

Technically, religion is a personal set or institutionalized system of religious attitudes, beliefs and practices. Studies show that religion (better defined in the research world as "faith in God") can make people happier and healthier. But religion can also be deceptive—and even deadly. Indeed, wars have been fought and multitudes have died over religion. Many who perished in those battles never had a chance to hear the saving Gospel of Christ. Look no further than radical Islam for modern-day examples.

Whether in the Middle East or elsewhere over the world, religious wars—holy wars—begin in the spirit. "We do not wrestle against flesh and blood, but against principalities, against powers, against the rulers of the darkness of this age, against spiritual hosts of wickedness in the heavenly places" (Ephesians 6:12). When we fail to win the war in the heavenlies, the war manifests in the natural realm. Jezebel is running rampant in the world today because we have allowed this principality to have its way. Collectively as the Body of Christ, we have not exercised the believer's authority to bind this wickedness. We have tolerated Jezebel—and its religion.

Getting to Know Jezebel's Gods

To understand how the Jezebel deception works we need to understand Jezebel's gods. Jezebel is religious indeed, but it is not Jehovah God it is worshiping. King Ahab and Queen Jezebel gave their children Hebrew names, but I believe it was more a case of being politically correct than a way to honor the God of the Hebrews.

Jezebel may throw the name of Jehovah (or Jesus) into the mix, but this is just lip service. As Jesus said, "These people draw near to Me with their mouth, and honor Me with their lips, but their heart is far from Me" (Matthew 15:8). Not everyone who names the name of Jesus has a heart for Him. The New Age movement is a prime example. Many New Agers quote the teachings of Buddha alongside the teachings of Jesus with equal authority.

In just the same manner, Queen Jezebel worshiped multiple gods. Jezebel served Ashtoreth and Baal primarily, gods spun out of the Babylonian system. Some scholars suggest that the spiritual entities knows as Baal and Tammuz—the child that Semiramis bore and claimed to be the reborn Nimrod—are one and the same.

Ashtoreth, the Queen of Heaven, is the female counterpart to Baal. Ashtoreth was the high goddess of Canaan, the goddess of love and war. According to the *International Standard Bible Encyclopedia*, prostitution was practiced in the name of Ashtoreth. This spirit delivered oracles to prophetesses in its temples.

Baal is known as the god of prophetic divination. The spirit of Baal leads people into idolatry just as it led the Israelites into idolatry when Moses was on the mountain talking with God. Do you remember how the children of Israel made a molten calf to worship? That was the spirit of Baal they were worshiping (see Exodus 32:8). Prophets of Baal, then, offer prophetic utterances that lead people into idolatry. In other words, they lead their followers away from God and toward selfish personal motives.

Jezebel's Modern Cults

I want to discuss several Christian cults here, because these types of religions are powered by the Jezebel spirit. Anyone on a quest for deeper faith who turns to false religious like Hinduism, Shintoism or Buddhism is aware that these religions are not Christian. Choosing to follow the gods of these religions means turning away from the truth of the Bible.

Christian cults are much more deceptive, in one sense, because their adherents usually believe they are being obedient to the teachings of Scripture. These groups often promote sexual and idolatrous behavior, and, as such, they are a prime destination for Jezebel. Followers are enticed with words that sound orthodox, and gradually deception takes hold of them. The world watches amazed as cult leaders drive their members into terrible actions.

David Koresh and Jim Jones, whom we will observe in this chapter, are two prominent examples, having orchestrated mass suicides. If you look closely at the inner workings of these cults, you will find the Jezebel deception. You will see that none other than Jezebel morphed the Gospel into a religion of idolatry and sexual immorality.

As you read about just a few of Jezebel's cults in the following pages, consider that none of these religious movements started off seething with idolatry and sexual immorality. Rather, the idolatry and sexual immorality were a result of the cult's adopting Jezebel's Babylonian religion. As the leaders of these various movements walked further and further into darkness, led either by the devil or the evil in their own hearts, they opened the door wide to the Jezebel deception. Gradually their followers began to idolize the leadership and participated in vile sexual acts, whether consensually or by force.

"Reforming" the Gospel

Led by David Koresh, the Branch Davidians emerged from a Protestant reform movement first begun in 1930. Victor Houteff, a Bulgarian immigrant who was expelled from the Greek Orthodox Church, had a "new revelation" and decided that his newly chosen denomination, the Seventh-day Adventist Church, should receive it. He outlined that revelation in a book called *The Shepherd's Rod: The 144,000—A Call for Reformation.*

When the Seventh-day Adventist Church rejected his revelation and excommunicated him (note: this marked the second time he was disfellowshiped from a body of believers), Houteff formed his own religion bent on "reforming" the Seventh-day Adventist Church. Houteff's unwelcomed revelation sought to prepare God's people for the impending doom of prophecy in Ezekiel 9.

In the 1950s, Houteff died and his church split. The Branch Davidians emerged under the leadership of Benjamin Roden. Roden's wife, Lois, claimed a "divine revelation" in 1977. Sound familiar? Founder Houteff had a "new revelation" and Lois Roden followed up with a "divine revelation." Both of these religious leaders were in serious error. They were not merely introducing new revelation; they were introducing new doctrine. Divine revelation from the Holy Spirit always points us toward Jesus and aligns with the written Word of God. The testimony of Jesus is the spirit of prophecy (see Revelation 19:10). Lois's revelation was not so divine.

Jezebel-Inspired False Doctrine?

Lois's doctrine taught that the Holy Spirit was feminine in gender, and, thus, she preached the concept of the Trinity as God the Father, God the Mother and God the Son. This claim gave Lois self-justification, as a woman, to assume a leadership position in the church. Perhaps Lois did not realize that she did not need false doctrine to assume leadership in the church—she just needed a divine calling.

Many women have been called through the ages to positions of leadership in the Body of Christ. Here are just a few from the last century. In the 1920s Aimee Semple McPherson founded the International Church of the Foursquare Gospel and built the 5,300-seat Angelus Temple. Kathryn Kuhlman started holding miracle services in 1948. Marilyn Hickey entered ministry in the

1960s, and was still having impact on the world in her eighties. Those are just a few examples of the female ministry pioneers who showed the world that the Holy Spirit gives women authority in the Church.

Could it be possible that Lois, far from following the Holy Spirit, received revelation from the spirit of Jezebel? In *Prophets of the Apocalypse: David Koresh & Other American Messiahs* (Baker, 1994), Kenneth R. Samples writes this: "She arrived at this novel bit of 'new light' through a 1977 vision that happened while she was studying Revelation 18:1 at 2 a.m. one day. In her words, she looked out her bedroom window and saw a 'vision of a shining, silver angel fly by.'"

It grieves me to see how many people point to angels in false prophetic revelation. Angelic encounters can certainly be authentic, but too many people in the Body of Christ are claiming angelic revelations outside the boundaries of Scripture. And it is dangerous. Paul warned, "For Satan himself transforms himself into an angel of light. Therefore it is no great thing if his ministers also transform themselves into ministers of righteousness, whose end will be according to their works" (2 Corinthians 11:14–15).

When Lois's husband died the following year, her son George claimed rights as the prophet of the church. Lois fought him in a secular court of law—something the apostle Paul discourages in 1 Corinthians 6:1–8—and won a permanent injunction against her son's presidency. In this way, the power-hungry Lois took over the church and continued teaching her "revelation" that the Holy Spirit is female.

Lois received international recognition, including an award from the Dove Foundation for the magazine she published. Could it be possible that a Jezebel spirit took control of the Branch Davidians, perpetuating false doctrine about the Holy Spirit, the very spirit of prophecy?

Jezebel's Fornication

The manifestation of the Jezebel spirit intensified when Vernon Howell, later known as David Koresh, discovered the Branch Davidians. Koresh, 24, moved in with Lois, 67, and became romantically involved with her. Lois gave the young man opportunities to teach in the church, and he assumed leadership, declaring himself as "the Seventh Angel" from the book of Revelation. Soon, Koresh married a fourteen-year-old girl.

Lois, perhaps feeling her authority threatened, stood up in a meeting and told the congregation about the sordid sexual escapades she had had with her young live-in disciple. But by this time the congregation was idolizing Koresh as Lois's successor. The Branch Davidians accepted Koresh as the "Seventh Angel." Scripture says the seventh angel will sound a trumpet that will reveal "the mystery of God" (Revelation 10:7), and that when the seventh angel pours out his bowl into the air, "a loud voice [will come] out of the temple of heaven, from the throne, saying, 'It is done!'" (Revelation 16:17).

Koresh rose to power and married several women before declaring that all unmarried women in the compound were his wives. Eventually, Koresh declared that all men in the compound must also surrender their wives to him. Koresh used intimidation, verbal abuse and threats of his followers losing their salvation as a means to coerce the women into having sex with him. In 1993, Koresh—and many of his followers—died in a mass-suicide fire when the United States Bureau of Alcohol, Tobacco and Firearms tried to execute a search warrant at the Branch Davidian compound outside of Waco, Texas.

This is the Jezebel agenda. Control and manipulation are a means to lead people into idolatry and sexual immorality—and eventually death. Jezebel played all her cards and won this hand in Waco. According to the Department of Justice, 75 people died inside the compound, including 25 children.

"Flirty Fishing"

The Branch Davidians are not the only modern-day example of a cult that Jezebel dominated. The Peoples Temple, under leader Jim Jones, was also characterized by idolatry and sexual immorality. According to Rebecca Moore's *A Sympathetic History of Jonestown: The Moore Family's Involvement in Peoples Temple* (Edwin Mellen, 1985), "the adulation and worship Jim Jones' followers gave him was idolatrous. . . . Our children and members of Peoples Temple placed in Jim Jones the trust, and gave to him the loyalty that we were created to give God alone."

Accusations of sexual immorality followed Jim Jones's ministry as early as 1965. Those accusations continued to haunt him into the early 1970s, and, according to Ruth A. Tucker's *Another Gospel: Cults, Alternative Religions, and the New Age Movement* (Zondervan, 2004), Jones moved his twenty thousand followers to Guyana to escape the criticism of the press. Some reports document that Jones took his sexual immorality even further than Koresh, sodomizing members of his congregation to prove they were homosexual. Nearly one thousand of his followers died in 1978 by cyanide or gunshot.

Joseph Smith, founder of the Church of Jesus Christ of Latter-day Saints, quoted a "divine revelation" to incorporate polygamy into his Mormon religion. Historians debate how many wives Smith had. Sexual immorality.

Then there's The Family International, also known as the Children of God. The Family practiced an evangelistic method known as "flirty fishing" that used sex to win souls. In fact, the United Kingdom's High Court of Justice ruled there was "widespread sexual abuse of young children and teenagers by adult members of The Family." Sexual immorality.

Jezebel's Reprobate Religion

Can you see the Jezebel influence in these cults? If you are looking for a spirit of control alone, you might miss it. The Jezebel deception often works to lead people into idolatry and sexual immorality in the name of Jesus. Once Jezebel gains a stronghold in any ministry, the manifestations become more visible. How does it happen?

Consider the times we are living in. Consider the enormous influence the spirit of Jezebel has on our society. And consider the progression of sin. We noted earlier Paul's warning to Timothy: "Now the Spirit expressly says that in latter times some will depart from the faith, giving heed to deceiving spirits and doctrines of demons, speaking lies in hypocrisy, having their own conscience seared with a hot iron" (1 Timothy 4:1–2).

Romans 1 outlines a strategy Jezebel uses to woo believers into her murderous grip. Not only is Jezebel a deceiving spirit promoting doctrines of demons, but also it is a patient principality. Jezebel will take its time to seduce someone deeper and deeper into error. Jezebel's overarching strategy in wickedness is to repress the truth. It will then replace the truth with its reprobate religion.

The Jezebel deception starts with idolatry: "Although they knew God, they did not glorify Him as God, nor were thankful, but became futile in their thoughts, and their foolish hearts were darkened" (Romans 1:21). When we know God and do not glorify Him or thank Him for who He is and what He has done, we are behaving like mere fools who do not know God—and we are not walking in the reverential fear of the Lord who called us "out of darkness into His marvelous light" (1 Peter 2:9). When we turn our worship away from God to ourselves or something else, it is idolatry.

Exchanging God's Truth for Jezebel's Lie

You can see the progression of the Jezebel deception in Romans 1. Of course, these verses do not apply solely to Jezebel; the passage reveals the slow and deadly progression of any sin. As such, they give us excellent clarification of the working of evil. Again, Romans 1 could be considered a high-level tactical outline for Jezebel's patient work. Let's read on.

> Therefore God also gave them up to uncleanness, in the lusts of their hearts, to dishonor their bodies among themselves, who exchanged the truth of God for the lie, and worshiped and served the creature rather than the Creator.
>
> Romans 1:24–25

God is, of course, full of mercy and long-suffering. But when we refuse to repent for our idolatry and lusts—when we abandon the truth we know for a convenient lie and worship another god—our loving Creator will eventually allow us to pursue that uncleanness. We have free will. Even if it hurts His heart, He will not usurp our choices.

> For this reason God gave them up to vile passions. For even their women exchanged the natural use for what is against nature. Likewise also the men, leaving the natural use of the woman, burned in their lust for one another, men with men committing what is shameful, and receiving in themselves the penalty of their error which was due.
>
> Romans 1:26–27

Romans 1 shows clearly how idolatry can lead to sexual immorality. First, the people did not glorify God—they worshiped idols (the creature rather than the Creator). Then, they walked into the realm of sexual immorality. Although Jezebel's influence is not limited to homosexual activity—any form of sexual immorality will do—the Jezebel deception is what causes gay, lesbian, bi-sexual and transgender people to believe that they can willfully embrace abominations—never declaring war on the temptation—and still enter the Kingdom of heaven (see 1 Corinthians 6:9). God loves homosexuals, but He will not tolerate willful, unrepentant sexual immorality forever.

Let's read on to the next stage of this sinful progression.

> And even as they did not retain God in their knowledge, God gave them over to a debased mind, to do those things which are not fitting; being filled with all unrighteousness, sexual immorality, wickedness, covetousness, maliciousness; full of envy, murder, strife, deceit, evil-mindedness; they are whisperers, backbiters, haters of God, violent, proud, boasters, inventors of evil things, disobedient to parents, undiscerning, untrustworthy, unloving, unforgiving, unmerciful; who, knowing the righteous judgment of God, that those who practice such things are deserving of death, not only do the same but also approve of those who practice them.
>
> Romans 1:28–32

This is where Jezebel's religion wants to claim every born-again believer. The Jezebel deception is prevalent in secular society, but it is not satisfied with this. Jezebel wants to convert children of God into eunuchs who ultimately become haters of God. There are many steps along the way to a reprobate mind, and anyone can repent and turn back to our loving God at any time. But anyone who moves deeper into the Jezebel deception finds that it becomes gradually more difficult to sense the Holy Spirit's conviction, and eventually the wages of sin are death (see Romans 6:23).

Jezebel Infiltrates the Prophetic Movement

By now, you understand Jezebel's religion, how it has influenced cults and how Jezebel will lead its followers toward its wicked end. But have you considered the more subtle ways that Jezebel has infiltrated the modern prophetic movement in the authentic Christian Church? We know that the spirit of Jezebel largely controlled the prophetic movement in Old Testament Israel. But can you discern Jezebel's influence over some prophetic camps in the Church today?

Think about it for a minute. Some prophetic superstars are exalted to demigod status. That, beloved, is idolatry. People rush to conferences and stand in prayer lines with $1,000 offerings hoping for a prophetic word, rather than seeking God Himself for direction. It is a hyped-up Holy Ghost sale. But the Holy Ghost is not for sale—nor are His gifts. The Bible says covetousness (the inordinate desire for wealth or possessions) is idolatry (see Colossians 3:5). This idolatry can lead prophets straight into the clutches of Jezebel's sexual immorality, as we saw in Romans 1. It is all part of Jezebel's religion—and Jezebel's religion breeds false prophets.

In His Sermon on the Mount, Jesus closed with a word about false prophets. He warned listeners to beware of false prophets, who come dressed in sheep's clothing, but inwardly are ravenous wolves. In other words, they look and sound like the real thing but their motives are murderous. Jesus said we would know false prophets by their fruit. But then He said something shocking:

> "Not everyone who says to Me, 'Lord, Lord,' shall enter the kingdom of heaven, but he who does the will of My Father in heaven. Many will say to Me in that day, 'Lord, Lord, have we not prophesied in Your name, cast out demons in Your name, and done many wonders in Your name?' And then I will declare to them, 'I never knew you; depart from Me, you who practice lawlessness!'"
>
> Matthew 7:21–23

Prophesying, casting out devils and doing wonders? Those key words describe the prophetic ministry. Jezebel wants to lead—and, in fact, is leading—some in the modern prophetic movement into the practice of lawlessness. These are people who prophesy with great accuracy, cast out devils with great success and perform miracles in the name of Jesus. Imagine the shock when some of these ministers try to enter the Kingdom of heaven only to discover that they have been deceived into believing a false religion. Jezebel has duped them.

6

Are We Glorifying Jezebel?

Some people will always remember where they were when Neil Armstrong took "one giant leap for mankind" on a televised moonwalk. Others will always remember where they were when Walter Cronkite announced, tearfully, that John F. Kennedy was dead. Still others will always remember where they were when two jetliners flew into the iconic World Trade Center on September 11, 2001.

I am too young to remember the first two incidents, and I could never forget 9/11. But there was another moment in my life, so dramatic to me personally, that it left an indelible mark in my memory bank. I will always remember the moment when I first realized that Jezebel had targeted my life for destruction. It was one of those life-changing "aha" moments; a flash of understanding that opened my eyes to the deadly operations of this principality and its witchcrafts.

Here is the condensed version: A young man in my church was interested in me romantically, but I did not return the affection.

Hoping to spark some sort of twisted competition for his favor, he made up grandiose (and perverted) lies about having a relationship with my best friend. When his lie was exposed, and I made it clear that he must exit my life at all levels, he instead began stalking me.

Eventually, one of the pastors asked him not to return to our church because he was operating in a seducing, controlling spirit and would not receive counsel. He was unstable and it was getting scarier all the time. When I say he was stalking me, I mean it literally. He was under the influence of a Jezebel spirit. It was not the first time Jezebel had targeted me. It was just the first time I understood who the enemy was.

What I now refer to as this "Jezebel revelation" was at first liberating. The Jezebel revelation explained the nature of spiritual attacks I had experienced for decades. When I finally discerned the Jezebelic assignment against my life, evident in this young man's threats, my mouth literally dropped open. In an instant, I understood why the enemy had made it a mission to kill me, steal from me and otherwise bring destruction into my life.

Falling into Jezebel's Ditch

I will be honest. At first I felt somewhat important that Jezebel would pick on "little old me." As I educated myself with what materials I could find on this principality, I grew confident in my ability to identify a Jezebel spirit—and I had the faith to overcome. But before too long, however, I was unwittingly glorifying Jezebel, and I did not even have a full understanding of what I was battling.

While I will always remember the moment I got the revelation of the existence of Jezebel, I will also remember how far out of balance I had gotten with that revelation. As I mentioned, it was liberating to understand that Jezebel was working to steal, kill and destroy through a young man who was stalking me. When I discovered the name *Jezebel*, I was no longer buffeting the air, so to speak, because I had identified the enemy.

In my immaturity, however, and based on incomplete understanding, I waged war against Jezebel and began to blame this spirit for everything that went wrong in my life. I thought every obstacle was Jezebel. So I went around "binding" that spirit every time something failed to go my way. I rose up against Jezebel in spiritual warfare every time I encountered someone who I thought was trying to control me or manipulate me. I put Jezebel under my feet every morning when I woke up with a list of confessions to ward her off as if she were some sort of daylight vampire.

When my computer crashed: "I bind you, Jezebel. You nasty witch!" When my tire went flat: "I bind you, Jezebel. You nasty witch!" When I had a bad day: "I bind you, Jezebel. You nasty witch!" Looking back, I see the danger. But this is what I was taught to do by the spiritual leaders around me, who often raised their voices against this evil spirit to the point of becoming hoarse.

I began to realize that this was an exercise in the flesh and reaped no fruit: All the binding never seemed to keep Jezebel at bay. The prophets in that church had dreams of red-haired Jezebels trying to take over the youth group, and visions of Jezebels with black hats carrying guns into the church to shoot the pastor, and "proof" of Jezebels infiltrating various departments in the church. It seemed as though all the shouting just brought greater attacks and fewer victories. Jezebel was the center of constant warfare. The church had developed a Jezebel culture.

Jezebel was behind every doorknob. If someone got sick, it was Jezebel's witchcrafts. If someone did not want to come to church, it was Jezebel's imaginations. If someone had a strong opinion that did not agree with the pastor's, it was Jezebel's control. Jezebel was exalted, and few realized that Jezebel had taken over the church.

Soon it became evident. Where Jezebel rules in a church, manifestations of immorality and idolatry are prevalent. I have since seen many instances of this: worship team members having affairs, translators going to the mission fields high on drugs, spiritual abuse stripping people of the knowledge of who they are in Christ.

Should We Ignore It?

The Jezebel spirit is alive and well, and busy working out its agenda. But ignoring the spirit of Jezebel is to violate Scripture. Jesus did not ignore the dark side. Jesus pointed to the devil's work in the parable of the sower (see Luke 8:12), and John makes it clear that Jesus came to "destroy the works of the devil" (see 1 John 3:8). Peter tells us to be sober and vigilant for a good reason: Your adversary the devil walks around like a roaring lion, seeking someone to devour (see 1 Peter 5:8). Paul talks about people falling into the devil's snare (see 1 Timothy 3:7), and how the devil takes them captive to do his will (see 2 Timothy 2:26). We are supposed to resist the devil (see James 4:7) and not be ignorant of his devices (see 2 Corinthians 2:10–11).

We can apply all those Scriptures to the Jezebel spirit. Jesus did not ignore "that woman Jezebel." He warned us about Jezebel so that we could wage war against it. So, again, to decide consciously to ignore this spirit would be to violate Scripture. We need teaching that exposes Jezebel and equips the saints to defeat it. But to focus excessively on Jezebel and other spiritual warfare teachings at the expense of a balanced Gospel is also an error.

Let me make a bold statement: Some camps in the Body of Christ today are not only opening the door to Jezebel's influence, they are actually glorifying this evil spirit. No, the preacher does not stand up and approve of Jezebel's works. Quite the opposite: He condemns Jezebel. But if the preacher talks about Jezebel's power and cunning often enough, the sheep soon give this principality the preeminence that belongs to Jesus. In other words, some preachers are exalting Jezebel. In most cases this is done in ignorance, but I believe some do it for profit. Jezebel is big business.

What Spirit Are We Glorifying?

God makes it clear that He will not give His glory to another: "I will not give My glory to another [by permitting the worshipers of idols to triumph over you]" (Isaiah 48:11, AMPLIFIED). When we are worshiping anyone—or anything—other than God, we are giving His glory to another. When we engage in idolatry of any form, we are giving His glory to another. When we spend more time teaching, preaching, praying against and prophesying about Jezebel than we do worshiping God, we are giving His glory to another.

Despite biblical warning about idolatry, some preachers have set up Jezebel as a demonic rock star to be both despised and revered. Some use Jezebel as a popular sermon topic that unites the congregation against a common enemy. Some have learned that articles on Jezebel drive traffic to their websites. Some have discovered that books and CDs on Jezebel are strong sellers, so they have sliced and diced the topic into series that line their pockets with profits.

Jezebel feeds on the glory. Consider this: Glorifying Jezebel is a form of idolatry. The simplest definition of *idol* is "a false god." The dictionary defines *idol* as a "representation or symbol of an object of worship." Another definition is "pretender, imposter." Yet another definition is "an object of extreme devotion, a false conception." In some churches, Jezebel takes a preeminent position not because of what the principality is actually doing, but because of what the congregation *assumes* it is doing. In some Spirit-filled churches today, the devil and demons get more glory than the Father, Son and Holy Spirit.

I remember visiting one church service just as the praise and worship music was beginning. The worship leader began screaming at the devil and sweating something fierce. Loud, pounding music accompanied him. Over and over he "bound" Jezebel, witchcraft, a spirit of religion and other demons.

This was not just an introductory worship segment; it was a running theme throughout the service. Can you imagine the impression it made on lost souls walking through the door looking for Jesus? We heard very little about Jesus, save the binding of demons in His name. Song after song spoke of the enemy and our authority over him, at the expense of giving honor and glory to our King. The atmosphere was more like a battlefield than a sanctuary. It was too much for me—and that is saying a lot since I will be the first one to show up at a spiritual warfare meeting.

One of the greeters must have seen a look of concern on my face. She came over and whispered, "This is a special service because of Halloween and all the interference from witches."

I gave the church the benefit of the doubt and returned on another occasion. After all, witches are working overtime during Halloween, and there are times and seasons to focus on spiritual warfare. But this church was not merely in a time or season. Once more the service was devil-binding and demon-focused. At times, Jesus was lifted up. But the praise, preaching, prayer and prophesying were focused on various demons, with Jezebel having top billing.

The Danger of Exalting Demons

Let me say it again: Rather than exalting Christ from the platform, some churches have fallen into the trap of exalting demons. They probably do not realize what they are doing, but they are doing it just the same. If it is not Jezebel, it is Ahab, Absalom, religion, witchcraft, some other named demon or Satan himself. These same churches wonder why members of the congregation are falling into immorality, idolatry and other sin. They wonder why ungodly imaginations and terrible sicknesses are manifesting instead of true prophetic utterances and divine healing.

I submit to you that, to some extent, we get what we preach. Put another way, faith comes by hearing, so the messages we hear shape what we believe. We also become more aware of what we are focused on. If we are in the market for a new red Toyota, we will notice every new red Toyota on the road. With that in mind, if we are preaching Jesus, Jesus will draw us to Himself (see John 12:32). We will have more faith in Jesus, and we will more often notice the work of Jesus in our lives.

What happens, then, if our churches preach more about principalities, powers, rulers of the darkness of this world, and spiritual wickedness in high places than they preach about Jesus? What happens if we are preaching more about the power of demons than the power of God? Those messages shape what we believe and what we focus on, and suspicion of devils behind every doorknob may replace true discernment.

Don't get me wrong. I believe in spiritual warfare and I believe in using my Christ-given authority to bind the spirit of Jezebel and any other spirit that stands in the way of God's will. I believe we need teaching on Jezebel and other spiritual warfare topics. But when it gets out of balance and people are learning more about evil than about God, the door is being opened for deception. We become like whatever we glorify; we morph into the image of what we worship. If we are glorifying false gods like Jezebel, I believe we can take on those characteristics.

This is biblical. When the Israelites worshiped idols, they became like their idols that could neither perceive nor see nor hear (see Deuteronomy 29:4). God sent Isaiah, saying,

> "Go, and tell this people: 'Keep on hearing, but do not understand; keep on seeing, but do not perceive.' Make the heart of this people dull, and their ears heavy, and shut their eyes; lest they see with their eyes, and hear with their ears, and understand with their heart, and return and be healed."
>
> Isaiah 6:9–10

The confession of our mouths (as well as our choices and actions) gives either God or demons dominion over us. When believers confess the power of Jezebel, they may neglect the power of Jesus. We should know our enemy, but we should not exalt our enemy. Glorifying demons would be dangerous enough if Jezebel were merely a spirit of control and manipulation. But when we understand that Jezebel is the spirit of seduction that leads us into immorality and idolatry, the issue becomes even more serious.

A Jezebel Culture

The spirit of Jezebel would actually prefer that you never know it is operating in your midst. But once you see the Jezebel spirit manifesting, it wants all your attention. Too many Spirit-filled believers are just as I once was—out of balance and giving Jezebel far too much credit. Basically, I went from the ditch of ignorance about Jezebel to the ditch of excess.

Peter wrote this: "Be well balanced (temperate, sober of mind), be vigilant and cautious at all times; for that enemy of yours, the devil, roams about like a lion roaring [in fierce hunger], seeking someone to seize upon and devour" (1 Peter 5:8, AMPLIFIED). When we focus too much on Jezebel—or on spiritual warfare in general—then we risk building a spiritual warfare culture instead of a Jesus culture.

If we are living in nonstop warfare with no seasons of rest, I submit to you that something is wrong. Jesus said, "Come to Me, all you who labor and are heavy-laden and overburdened, and I will cause you to rest. [I will ease and relieve and refresh your souls]" (Matthew 11:28, AMPLIFIED). When the spiritual warfare gets intense—and it does get intense during certain seasons—we can go to Jesus. "He who dwells in the secret place of the Most High shall remain stable and fixed under the shadow of the Almighty [Whose power no foe can withstand]" (Psalm 91:1, AMPLIFIED).

"No foe" includes Jezebel. The writer of Hebrews put it this way:

> Therefore we also, since we are surrounded by so great a cloud of witnesses, let us lay aside every weight, and the sin which so easily ensnares us, and let us run with endurance the race that is set before us, looking unto Jesus, the author and finisher of our faith, who for the joy that was set before Him endured the cross, despising the shame, and has sat down at the right hand of the throne of God.
>
> Hebrews 12:1–2

The Lord promises to keep us in perfect peace if our minds are focused on Him (see Isaiah 26:3). It is hard to walk in peace when you are fearful of Jezebel's attacks around every corner.

Discerning When to War

The Preacher said that there is a time of war and a time of peace (see Ecclesiastes 3:8). Mature saints—who are not in a spiritual ditch—can discern the season and respond appropriately.

Yes, there is a season when kings go to war (see 2 Samuel 11:1). If you do not go to war when you are called to go to war, then you are out of God's will and you open the door for the enemy to tempt you into sin. If you do not go to war against the Jezebel spirit—if you tolerate that spirit Jezebel, if you give it any opportunity in your life—this principality may very well seduce you into sexual immorality and idolatry.

We saw this happen in the life of King David. In the spring— the time when kings went out to battle—David sent Joab to lead Israel into war against the people of Ammon. David was commander in chief of the army and a mighty warrior. David should have been the one to lead Israel into battle, but he gave his authority to Joab. David should have run to the battle line as he did when he conquered Goliath, but he handed the job to others. David remained at Jerusalem. His army may have conquered the Ammonites, but the Jezebel spirit conquered him in that season through the lust of the flesh.

You know the story. While his men were out fighting, David was taking a nap. It has been said the devil will find work for idle hands to do. David proved the point as he strolled on the roof of his palace. Rather than fasting and praying for his army, David gazed on a woman bathing. Rather than walking away, I believe he listened to Jezebel's whispers and gave in to the lust of the eyes. David asked about the woman, and was told she was the wife of Uriah the Hittite. The fact that she was a married woman did not deter David from entering into sexual immorality.

We see nothing in the Word about David repenting immediately afterward, either. Instead, when he found out that Bathsheba was pregnant, he arranged to have Uriah, a faithful soldier in his army, murdered. Who do you think was whispering in David's ear to commit murder? Could it be possible that Jezebel, the spirit of idolatry and immorality—the same spirit that seduced him into idolatry through the lust of his eyes and the lust of his flesh—suggested the "solution"?

As you consider this, also consider that if Jezebel can seduce David, a man after God's own heart, then it can seduce anyone who does not walk in line with God's Word. No one is exempt.

7

Persecuting True Prophets

The spirit of Jezebel is an enemy of the prophetic movement—as it has been for ages past. But Jezebel's assignment in the last days looks somewhat different from her agenda in 1 Kings.

Queen Jezebel merely wanted power and authority in the Kingdom of Israel. She worked to accomplish that, in part, by shutting down true prophetic voices in the land and usurping the king's authority. The spirit of Jezebel that is rising up in the last days wants more than power and authority in Israel: This principality wants authority over the nations.

Jezebel is not satisfied with wooing souls that are lost: Jezebel also wants to entice the saints out of the Kingdom of God and back into the kingdom of darkness from which they were delivered. Jezebel works to quench the fire of the Holy Spirit in the hearts of blood-bought believers and lead them straight into the fires of hell for eternity. Jezebel works to accomplish this by silencing the voices of the prophets. Once that is achieved, people can be enticed more easily into idolatry and sexual im morality, and their utter destruction.

In the Old Testament, we read that Queen Jezebel massacred many prophets of Jehovah. Obadiah, a man with a healthy fear of the Lord, hid one hundred true prophets in two caves, fifty in each cave (see 1 Kings 18:4). He was faithful to feed them bread and water, but this was probably just sufficient to keep them alive. All the while Jezebel's false prophets—450 prophets of Baal and 400 prophets of Asherah—were feasting at her table daily (see 1 Kings 18:19). During King Ahab's reign, the true prophetic voice in the land was largely cut off while false prophetic voices thrived.

While Queen Jezebel remained alive, the prophets stayed hidden in caves for fear of their lives. The spirit of Jezebel, alive today, also persecutes the prophets, albeit in different ways. First, it keeps them in hiding if they fall into sin because they are riddled with guilt. If Jezebel can entangle men and women of God—prophetic voices to this generation—with sexual sin, financial improprieties and other forms of idolatry, this wicked spirit can water down their messages and ultimately dismantle their platforms. After all, how credible is the prophet caught in sexual sin or fake healings or merchandising schemes?

Make no mistake, even if someone's sin is not exposed to the world, his internal struggles make him less effective in ministry and put him in danger of becoming Jezebel's puppet. Prophets who ignore the Holy Spirit's conviction of sin will eventually fall into a great deception.

Those prophets who repent of their sins often face a differ-ent kind of challenge, since humans do not always forgive and forget as quickly as our loving Lord God Almighty. Just look at the ministries of leaders who have fallen into sexual or financial sin. Even if they are restored, they tend to lose a large percent-age of their following and their ministries typically never fully recover from the scandal.

But even prophets who stand up for righteousness and refuse to fall under Jezebel's seductions are not without opposition: They will usually face persecution for preaching, teaching and living an uncompromising message. I speak out plenty about sexual immorality, for example, and I get harsh opposition from radical gay activists. Opposition can also come from churchgoers who may frown upon the prophet's cry to avoid the world's entertainment, like semi-pornographic broadcasts that air on prime-time television.

Remember Paul's words: "Yes, and all who desire to live godly in Christ Jesus will suffer persecution. But evil men and impostors will grow worse and worse, deceiving and being deceived" (2 Timothy 3:12–13).

Although prophetic ministers are in Jezebel's crosshairs, no one has to hold the office of prophet to be a target. If you are born again and Spirit-filled, you carry the prophetic voice of the Lord. You are a representative of the Kingdom of God. And Jezebel hates you.

Despising the Lord

We have all sinned and fallen short of the glory of God (see Romans 3:23). If we say that we have no sin, we deceive ourselves, and the truth is not in us (see 1 John 1:10). The point is, we all miss it more than we would like to admit, whether in word or deed, whether by commission or omission.

Although sin is sin, we tend to take some sins, like fornication, more seriously than some other sins—and I believe Scripture affirms that sexual sins are more serious than, say, a potty mouth. Paul explained it to the Corinthian church this way:

> There's more to sex than mere skin on skin. Sex is as much spiritual mystery as physical fact. As written in Scripture, "The two become one." Since we want to become spiritually one with the

Master, we must not pursue the kind of sex that avoids commitment and intimacy, leaving us more lonely than ever—the kind of sex that can never "become one."

There is a sense in which sexual sins are different from all others. In sexual sin we violate the sacredness of our own bodies, these bodies that were made for God-given and God-modeled love, for "becoming one" with another. Or didn't you realize that your body is a sacred place, the place of the Holy Spirit? Don't you see that you can't live however you please, squandering what God paid such a high price for? The physical part of you is not some piece of property belonging to the spiritual part of you. God owns the whole works. So let people see God in and through your body.

1 Corinthians 6:16–20, THE MESSAGE

In this sense, I believe that idolatry and immorality are more serious than gossiping or judging a brother or sister. Idolatry and immorality display disdain for the commandment of the Lord—and for the Lord Himself. When David was caught in adultery with Bathsheba, the prophet Nathan asked him a pointed question:

"Why have you despised the commandment of the LORD, to do evil in His sight? You have killed Uriah the Hittite with the sword; you have taken his wife to be your wife, and have killed him with the sword of the people of Ammon. Now therefore, the sword shall never depart from your house, because you have despised Me, and have taken the wife of Uriah the Hittite to be your wife."

2 Samuel 12:9–10

John Paul Jackson, author of *Unmasking the Jezebel Spirit*, noted in his Streams Ministries newsletter that anyone can fall prey to any sin, but prophetic people seem to be especially prone to sexual sin. Jackson reasons that this could be because of the heightened sensitivity that comes with the prophetic gift.

In many cases, prophetic individuals have experienced rejection so often that they harbor deep feelings of insecurity. . . .

Furthermore, they are prone to receive the acceptance of others with open arms, without maintaining an attitude of vigilance. Thus, a prophetic person who has not developed the characteristic of restraint becomes "open prey" for demonic torment and attraction. If [prophetic individuals] are insecure and if their identity lies in their spiritual gift, they will be prone to fall for anything or anyone who offers them love and acceptance.

Often, the temptation comes when they are experiencing a lull in their gift or ministry, and when they are feeling insecure. If their prophetic gift has formed the basis of their identity, whenever their prophetic insight wanes so does their identity. Therefore, the prophetic individual may fill the void with a temporary fix that will promise to fulfill their need to be valued. Sexual sin offers instant gratification and our social and moral climate today only further complicates this problem.*

Although we do not know for certain what caused David, himself a prophet, to fall into sexual sin with Bathsheba, I theorize that the Jezebel spirit enticed his flesh. We know that David was very sensitive to the Holy Spirit and was, therefore, as Jackson suggests, more sensitive to other spirits. Despite his special relationship with the Lord, and his repentance, David faced consequences for the sexual immorality and murder he committed. Indeed, sexual immorality and murder followed in his bloodline.

The Lord takes all sin seriously. He hates it all because of the damage sin causes to our souls. He loves us with a passion, and sin separates us from His holy presence. The Lord took David's

*John Paul Jackson, "When Prophetic People Come Under Attack by Satan," Streams Ministries International Newsletter, July 9, 2002, http://injesus.com/message-archives/church-and-ministry/mercyandtruthlist/when-prophetic-people-come-under-attack-by-satan-questions. Used by permission. Copyright 2002 Streams Ministries International, www.streamsministries.com.

sexual immorality to heart. Nathan equated it to despising the Lord. I believe when a Christian commits sexual immorality it hurts God's heart. Idolatry may be more subtle, but there is no mistaking sexual immorality. Sexual immorality is a serious sin. The more serious the sin, the greater the feelings of guilt and condemnation that follow in a sincere believer's heart.

And therein lies the trap: Believers struggling with guilt and condemnation—whether their sin is past or ongoing—do not feel qualified to move in the Spirit, and so forfeit their effectiveness in the Kingdom. In these cases the prophetic voice is shut down. Some believers manage to overcome the feelings of condemnation without overcoming the sin. In these cases, the prophetic voice is perverted. In other words, those who wallow in sin become ineffective oracles, and those who ignore the conviction become perverted voices.

And that is Jezebel's agenda. This principality first tries to shut down the prophetic voice. If that does not work, Jezebel is pleased to pervert it so that others either are led away from truth or refuse to listen to true prophetic utterances from the mouth of that vessel.

Prophets—indeed any believers—who continue in immorality eventually meet with a hot iron that sears their consciences (see 1 Timothy 4:1–2). They continue to lead Sunday morning worship even though they are getting drunk at the club every Saturday night. They continue to travel to the nations even though they are meeting prostitutes after the evening services. Ironically, they may even increase in works of ministry despite the fact that Jezebel is leading them. The deception is subtle, and few recognize these manifestations as the influence of this spirit. They may see the sin, but they are not connecting the dots that draw a picture of Jezebel.

And, as we have noted, some leaders know exactly what is going on but do not try to help these individuals see the danger.

They fail to deal with those in their midst who are living immoral, idolatrous lifestyles right under their noses. Whether they lack the courage to confront evil or want the "untouchables" to continue in their particular ministries, they tolerate Jezebel. The enemy will eventually lead conscience-seared believers into deeper and deeper deception as they continue to defile their spirits—even drawing them into the occult as they seek the supernatural. In the last days, false prophetic teaching will deceive many people, and love—the very thing by which Jesus said the world would know we are His disciples (see John 13:35)—will appear as a mound of ashes instead of a burning flame for Christ. Inspired by Satan himself, Jezebel is on the frontlines of this end time deception.

Jezebel's Payroll

Although Jezebel persecutes the prophets who refuse to bow to her idolatrous and immoral teachings, we see that Jezebel provides liberally for prophets who are willing to compromise their service to Jehovah in exchange for financial support and fame.

Observe the contrast. There were one hundred true prophets of God living in caves. The Bible does not offer any insight into the conditions within the cave, but it is safe to assume that those caves were not close to the accommodations in which some modern-day prophets rest their heads while traveling from church to church scooping up large offerings for questionable prophecies. (I am not against staying in a nice hotel. I am against fleecing the sheep to do it.)

The point is this: Caves are humble dwellings. The true prophets of God were hidden away in humble dwellings—probably dark, damp and uncomfortable—and they dined on bread and water. This was even more extreme than John the Baptist's lifestyle. At least John was free to roam about the wilderness as he searched for his locusts and honey without fear of Jezebel having him killed. The lifestyle of the one hundred prophets living in caves is also more extreme than Elijah's lowest point, where birds brought him bread and meat every morning and evening (see 1 Kings 17:6).

By contrast, Jezebel's prophets feasted like princes. These prophets were on the state payroll and lived the high life—all in exchange for telling Jezebel what she wanted to hear. Jezebel employed 450 prophets of Baal and 400 prophets of Asherah. For sake of argument, suppose that feeding each of them cost about $15 a day. Keeping these false prophets on the payroll would cost the Kingdom of Israel $12,750 a day. That is more than $4.6 million a year.

The Kingdom of Israel was essentially paying millions of dollars a year to support these false prophets. Money that belonged to God was used to turn God's very own people away from Him to other gods. How tragic! Now look at the Church in today's world. How many millions of dollars are unsuspecting saints paying Jezebel's prophets to tell them what they want to hear? How much of God's tithes and offerings are being used to turn people to idols? The Bible warns of this:

> "Thus says the Lord GOD: 'Everyone of the house of Israel who sets up his idols in his heart, and puts before him what causes him to stumble into iniquity, and then comes to the prophet, I the LORD will answer him who comes, according to the multitude of his idols.'"
>
> Ezekiel 14:4

In other words, God will let the prophet tell that person what he wants to hear. As Matthew Henry puts it, "According to the desire of their idols, He will give them up to their own hearts' lust, and leave them to themselves to be as bad as they have a mind to be, till they have filled up the measure of their iniquity."

It is a sad story. Instead of supporting missions so that the Gospel might be preached to every nation, some Christians are supporting false prophets who are drawing them—and many others—into idolatry by prophesying to the lusts of their hearts. Too many Christians are too dependent on prophets to tell them what God is saying in these times. I know this because people write me often asking for prophetic words (I do not engage in that practice), and it is easy to locate websites dedicated to selling personal prophecies. This is part of the Jezebel deception, and her way of diverting funds from true Kingdom work to accomplish her purposes.

Shunning Greed, Sexual Sin and Pride

I believe that wooing prophets with money, status or other perks is part of Jezebel's plan in the last days, just as it was in the Old Testament days. This is why it is so important for prophets to shun greed, immorality and pride. "For all that is in the world— the lust of the flesh, the lust of the eyes, and the pride of life—is not of the Father but is of the world" (1 John 2:16).

Think about it for a minute. Jezebel was supporting 850 false prophets. They probably felt superior to the true prophets of God who were hidden in caves. They were well-paid, well-fed, probably well-dressed and recognized in all the land as prophetic voices. Their prosperity and status validated them. They probably had no idea they were deceived. They may have even thought the true prophets of God were the ones who were walking in deception. That is often the way with strong delusion.

That is why it is so important to heed the apostle Paul's warning to

kill (deaden, deprive of power) the evil desire lurking in your members [those animal impulses and all that is earthly in you that is employed in sin]: sexual vice, impurity, sensual appetites, unholy desires, and all greed and covetousness, for that is idolatry (the deifying of self and other created things instead of God). It is on account of these [very sins] that the [holy] anger of God is ever coming upon the sons of disobedience (those who are obstinately opposed to the divine will).

Colossians 3:5–6, AMPLIFIED

This warning could be applied to the dangers of Jezebel in this hour. Paul specifically called out idolatry and immorality—and the Amplified translation slices and dices it several ways to make sure readers get the message loud and clear. *The Message* translation of these verses also helps bring home Paul's point—and my point about the dangers of getting caught up in greed:

Meanwhile, be content with obscurity, like Christ. And that means killing off everything connected with that way of death: sexual promiscuity, impurity, lust, doing whatever you feel like whenever you feel like it, and grabbing whatever attracts your fancy. That's a life shaped by things and feelings instead of by God. It's because of this kind of thing that God is about to explode in anger.

Please do not misunderstand. I am not against prophets—or any other servant of God—prospering or having God exalt his or her name in the world. Not at all. When we humble ourselves, God will exalt us (see James 4:10). When we sow, we will reap. But Jezebel works to woo prophets into greed and idolatry by tapping in to their carnal nature. This is why it is so vital to walk according to the Spirit and not according to the flesh:

For those who live according to the flesh set their minds on the things of the flesh, but those who live according to the Spirit, the things of the Spirit. For to be carnally minded is death, but to be spiritually minded is life and peace. Because the carnal mind is enmity against God; for it is not subject to the law of

God, nor indeed can be. So then, those who are in the flesh cannot please God.

Romans 8:5–8

Paul explained further how the flesh and the Spirit are contrary to one another. Right after he wrote that "the flesh lusts against the Spirit, and the Spirit against the flesh" (Galatians 5:17), he listed the works of the flesh:

> Now the works of the flesh are evident, which are: adultery, fornication, uncleanness, lewdness, idolatry, sorcery, hatred, contentions, jealousies, outbursts of wrath, selfish ambitions, dissensions, heresies, envy, murders, drunkenness, revelries, and the like; of which I tell you beforehand, just as I also told you in time past, that those who practice such things will not inherit the kingdom of God.

Galatians 5:19–21

Jezebel Buys Balaam's Loyalty

What does it look like when a prophet is influenced by Baal, one of Jezebel's gods? You can see the Jezebel influence clearly in the story of the prophet Balaam. When Moab's King Balak saw what Israel had done to the Amorites, and that his nation was scared and sick with dread, he sent messengers to Balaam. King Balak wanted Balaam to curse the Israelites—and he offered money to get the job done. The Bible calls it a diviner's fee (see Numbers 22:7).

Balaam sought the Lord—and he heard clearly from God. He let the king's messengers know that the Lord would not allow him to curse the Israelites. So Balaam rose in the morning and said to the princes of Balak, "Go back to your land, for the LORD has refused to give me permission to go with you" (Numbers 22:13).

But Jezebel did not give up that easily. Balak's next move was to offer Balaam honor in addition to mounds of money. Balaam once again sought the Lord. This decision showed how insensitive Balaam really was to the Lord's heart—and that there was an idol in his own heart that Jezebel could entice.

Did Balaam really think that if the Lord told him not to go curse the Israelites for money that it would be acceptable to curse them in exchange for money with a little honor on the side? Something in Balaam—likely pride and ambition in addition to greed—was hoping the Lord would repent and allow him to go. But it was Balaam who needed to repent.

Balaam said the right words out of one side of his mouth, "Though Balak were to give me his house full of silver and gold, I could not go beyond the word of the LORD my God, to do less or more" (Numbers 22:18). But out of the other side of his mouth he asked the princes to stay so he could inquire of the Lord again. Oh, how this must have grieved the Lord, who allowed him to follow the idols in his heart! The Lord told him to go with the messengers and speak the word of the Lord. But God was angry that he actually went (see Numbers 22:22).

Long story short, Balaam spoke blessings and not curses over the Israelites. Still, Jezebel did not give up. Balaam eventually gave in to the gold, silver and honor and offered Balak a strategy that would help him defeat Israel.

What was Balaam's counsel? For the women of Moab to seduce the men of Israel. Jezebel worked through Balaam to lead the Israelites into sexual immorality. Moses described that strategy in the book of Numbers:

> So Balaam rose and departed and returned to his place; Balak also went his way. Now Israel remained in Acacia Grove, and the people began to commit harlotry with the women of Moab. They invited the people to the sacrifices of their gods, and the people ate and bowed down to their gods. So Israel was joined

to Baal of Peor, and the anger of the LORD was aroused against Israel. Then the LORD said to Moses, "Take all the leaders of the people and hang the offenders before the Lord, out in the sun, that the fierce anger of the Lord may turn away from Israel." So Moses said to the judges of Israel, "Every one of you kill his men who were joined to Baal of Peor." . . . And those who died in the [subsequent] plague were twenty-four thousand.

Numbers 24:25; 25:1–5, 9

Moses described the punishment on the children of Israel in Numbers 31:16: "Look, these women caused the children of Israel, through the counsel of Balaam, to trespass against the LORD in the incident of Peor, [causing a] plague among the congregation of the LORD."

Every Israelite who committed sexual immorality with a Moabite woman was killed, either by hanging or plague—another example of how embracing Jezebel's teachings leads to death.

Jezebel's Prevalent Influence

Noteworthy is the fact that just as Jezebel is mentioned in the book of Revelation so is Balaam. Jesus chose to call out the compromise in the church in Pergamos:

> "These things says He who has the sharp two-edged sword: 'I know your works, and where you dwell, where Satan's throne is. And you hold fast to My name, and did not deny My faith even in the days in which Antipas was My faithful martyr, who was killed among you, where Satan dwells. But I have a few things against you, because you have there those who hold the doctrine of Balaam, who taught Balak to put a stumbling block before the children of Israel, to eat things sacrificed to idols, and to

111

commit sexual immorality. Thus you also have those who hold the doctrine of the Nicolaitans, which thing I hate.'"

Revelation 2:12–15

Sound familiar? Balaam and Jezebel are both associated with leading God's people into idolatry and sexual immorality. Jesus said the same thing about Jezebel in Revelation 2:20, just a few verses later. This is no coincidence. But what is the doctrine of the Nicolaitans? And who are the Nicolaitans?

Nicolaitans were followers of Nicolaus, a heretic, and were possibly a sect of the Gnostics. They practiced and taught immoral doctrines, including sexual licentiousness and that eating meats sacrificed to idols was lawful.

Although Balaam's story is outlined in the book of Numbers, Balaam's infamy runs through the Old and New Testaments. In addition to Numbers and Revelation, Balaam's wicked works are mentioned in Deuteronomy, Joshua, Nehemiah, Micah, 2 Peter and Jude. Do you think God is trying to tell us something here? Peter points to Balaam as one "who loved the wages of unrighteousness" (see 2 Peter 2:15), and Jude recalls Balaam as one who chased profit (see Jude 11). Covetousness is an idol, and Jezebel will use it to lead prophetic people and those who follow them into failure.

God Preserves a Remnant

Despite the immorality and idolatry in the Church today, the good news is that Jezebel is not winning. Not really. Elijah felt as though he was all alone in his battle against Jezebel and in his zeal for the Lord. But he was far from the only true prophet in the land. Beyond the one hundred prophets, God had thousands of other followers who refused to compromise His will.

You remember the scene in 1 Kings 19. Elijah was depressed, having fled Israel on foot after Jezebel threatened his life for slaying her false prophets at Mount Carmel. He rested for forty days and forty nights. When God asked Elijah what he was doing, the prophet gave Him an earful:

> "I have been very zealous for the LORD God of hosts; for the children of Israel have forsaken Your covenant, torn down Your altars, and killed Your prophets with the sword. I alone am left; and they seek to take my life."
>
> 1 Kings 19:10

Ultimately, the Lord told Elijah that help was on the way via Elisha and Jehu (see 1 Kings 19:17), and that he had "reserved seven thousand in Israel, all whose knees have not bowed to Baal, and every mouth that has not kissed him" (verse 18).

Despite the fact that prophetic voices to our generation are being caught in sexual and financial scandals, God still has a remnant that is faithful to Him. God has indeed set apart a remnant according to His grace—not by any special virtue of its members. I believe that Jezebel has "taken crafty counsel against [God's] people, and consulted together against [even His] sheltered ones" (Psalm 83:3), but God's grace will preserve the remnant.

Indeed, some churches in the book of Revelation shun Jezebel's influence. Jesus commended the church at Ephesus for identifying false apostles and for hating the deeds of the Nicolaitans. Jesus also commended the church at Smyrna, known as the persecuted church, and actually had nothing against them. The church in Philadelphia was also counted faithful. And there was a remnant in the church at Smyrna that had not given itself over to corruption.

God always preserves a remnant by His grace. Let us pray that the Lord will purify our hearts that we might be worthy of being part of that remnant. The alternative could be judgment.

8

Jezebel's Judgments

W hen we think of Jesus, we think of love, humility, mercy and long-suffering—and we should. God is love and Jesus is God. Scripture assures us that through "the LORD's mercies we are not consumed, because His compassions fail not. They are new every morning; great is [His] faithfulness" (Lamentations 3:22–23). We can rest in the fact that He will never break His covenant with us.

No, the Lord never leaves or forsakes us—but sometimes His children leave or forsake Him. And sometimes His children do not even realize that they are straying from the flock and into delusion. Indeed, that is part of the Jezebel deception. This drifting is typically slow and subtle as Jezebel seduces its victims with idols handcrafted to suit their hearts' desires. For some it is money. For others it is fame. For others it is various paths of immorality. Jezebel is patient. This principality watches and waits for the opportunity to snare believers. I believe the writer of Hebrews refers to this:

> Therefore we must give the more earnest heed to the things we
> have heard, lest we drift away. For if the word spoken through

angels proved steadfast, and every transgression and disobedience received a just reward, how shall we escape if we neglect
so great a salvation, which at the first began to be spoken by
the Lord, and was confirmed to us by those who heard Him.

Hebrews 2:1–3

Do not be deceived. Sin is crouching at your door. If you give
in to the temptations that Jezebel offers through idolatry and
immorality, God's long-suffering will eventually give way to His
judgment. Indeed, God has said "My Spirit shall not strive with
man forever" (Genesis 6:3). Matthew Henry's *Commentary*
offers insight into that verse:

> This comes in here as a token of God's displeasure at those who
> married strange wives; he threatens to withdraw from them his
> Spirit, whom they had grieved by such marriages, contrary to
> their convictions: fleshly lusts are often punished with spiritual
> judgments, the sorest of all judgments.

You cannot keep a covenant with Jesus and keep a covenant
with Jezebel at the same time. "No one can serve two masters;
for either he will hate the one and love the other, or else he will be
loyal to the one and despise the other" (Matthew 6:24). Jesus loves
you. When you stray from His heart—when you start marrying
strange wives, so to speak—His Holy Spirit will try to get your
attention. It is called conviction. The Holy Spirit will convict us of
sin, of righteousness and of judgment (see John 16:8). If the sinning
believer does not humble himself and pray and seek God's face
and turn from his wicked ways, God's judgment eventually comes.

Space to Repent

Again, Jesus is long-suffering. He endures patiently even our most
offensive sins for a season. The apostle Paul, known formerly

as Saul of Tarsus, is a good example of just how long-suffering Jesus is. Paul considered himself the chief of sinners because he had persecuted Christians. By his hand, many saints had been put into prison, and when they were put to death, he had cast his vote against them. The Bible says that Saul punished them often in every synagogue and compelled them to blaspheme. He even traveled to foreign cities to persecute them (see Acts 26:10–11). Saul was an orchestrator of evil. But Jesus is long-suffering.

One day while Saul was on the road to Damascus, Jesus revealed that He was the prophesied Lord, and that He was calling Saul to advance the Kingdom of God. Saul left that encounter blind and with an eternal decision to make (see Acts 9:3–7). He made the right decision. He repented—he gave up the idol of religion—and followed Jesus wholeheartedly for the rest of his life, despite enormous personal cost. But it took an encounter with God—an encounter that challenged his religious mind-set and left him blind for three days—to get through to him.

Jesus gave Saul space to repent because of the exceeding abundance of His grace, faith and love. If Saul had ignored that encounter with Jesus, I believe it would have meant devastating eternal consequences.

The great apostle understood the gravity of the moment. He later told his spiritual son, Timothy, "For this reason I obtained mercy, that in me first Jesus Christ might show all longsuffering, as a pattern to those who are going to believe on Him for everlasting life" (1 Timothy 1:16). In other words, Jesus wants us to know that He is long-suffering. Not so that we can freely sin, but so that we will run to Him when we do and receive grace to war against that sin. This kind of abundant grace, faith, love and mercy was also extended to the human Jezebel.

Make no mistake, Jesus gave Jezebel, the woman in the church at Thyatira, time to repent of her idolatry and immorality. Jesus specifically said:

"I gave her time to repent of her sexual immorality, and she did not repent. Indeed I will cast her into a sickbed, and those who commit adultery with her into great tribulation, unless they repent of their deeds. I will kill her children with death, and all the churches shall know that I am He who searches the minds and hearts. And I will give to each one of you according to your works."

Revelation 2:21–23

That does not sound like the loving picture we draw of Jesus, does it? Jesus was patient with Jezebel, but there comes a point when the grace runs out.

This is why false teachings on grace are so dangerous. I believe that we are in a dispensation of grace, and it follows, then, that I am slow to promote the idea that God is judging the nations at this time. In other words, we cannot attribute every hurricane and tornado to God's judgment on governments that are turning from Him. It is the enemy who comes to steal, kill and destroy. Jesus came to give us life (see John 10:10).

It might help us comprehend this if we substitute the word *judgment* with *discipline*. God is a loving Father, and He disciplines—rebukes and chastens—those He loves (see Revelation 3:19). God loves His people so much that He will sometimes use strict discipline to save their souls.

Saving Sammy's Soul

Sammy was serving faithfully in his local church in both the media ministry and youth ministry, but he was drinking just as faithfully. One of Sammy's team leaders warned him privately and repeatedly to stop the behavior and offered all kinds of help, from practical to spiritual. This young man repented verbally, but there was no fruit of that repentance.

Alcohol had become an idol in Sammy's life, but Jezebel was the spiritual seductress enticing him to let hard liquor eat away

118

at him—and his relationship with God. Sammy came from a broken home. His natural mother abandoned him when he was young. His father passed away a few years later. Jezebel offered him comfort through alcohol and pornography—and he accepted it. The church failed him, but his team leader, who knew only about the alcohol addiction, tried to help.

When it was clear that Sammy could not overcome the alcoholism on his own, the team leader informed the pastors. The pastors never addressed it, but instead decided to allow him to continue working in the ministries because no one else had the production skills required to get the radio broadcast completed each week. They did not want to remove him from the youth ministry because his stepmother, another good church volunteer, was in charge of the department.

Sammy was riding on the grace of God—and on the backs of pastors who cared more about performance than progress in Christ. These same pastors were under the influence of Jezebel, who probably whispered to them that he was just a normal young man sowing his oats and would grow out of it. We never grow out of sin. We never grow out of bondage. But we can repent and be delivered.

Sammy continued drinking even while doing the work of the ministries until members of the congregation reported smelling alcohol on his breath during Sunday morning service. The pastors then had no choice but to acknowledge it. They talked to him privately, but they allowed him to continue in his ministry. And Sammy continued his immoral behavior. He kept going to church with alcohol on his breath, though better masked with breath mints and too much cologne. Soon, some began to suspect that he was also involved in homosexuality.

Sammy was 35 years old and still living at home with his stepmother when the grace of God finally waned. Sammy got fired from his job and could not find employment for more than two years. As the evidence of sin kept pouring in, parents of the youth in the church did not want him around their kids anymore. Some even left the church to put their children in a more stable and safer environment.

Sammy became nocturnal, staying up all night watching pornography on his computer and drinking hard liquor—then sleeping half the day. The church's radio ministry dried up. People started leaving the congregation in droves. I believe God led those people away, in part, because the pastors would not deal with the sin—or repent themselves for tolerating Jezebel.

Remarkably, Sammy did finally break free from the bondages of idolatry and immorality, but it was not until he left that Jezebel-controlled church and its powerful influence over him. He moved to another city and, through hard work and good counsel, Sammy finally got his life back in line with Christ.

Eli's House Is Judged

Spiritual leaders have a mandate not to tolerate Jezebel and its efforts to control and manipulate the flocks in their care—to seduce them—into idolatry and immorality. Spiritual leaders have a responsibility to train up their spiritual children in the way they should go—and teach them the way they should not go. Remember Eli.

The Bible says that Eli's sons, Hophni and Phinehas, were corrupt and that they did not know the Lord. How could the sons of a priest not know the Lord? The answer, at least in this case, is evident: Eli did not stand in his role as father and spiritual leader. He allowed Jezebel to usurp his authority in the family unit. As a result, Eli's sons were tightly in Jezebel's clutches.

The Bible says Eli's sons "lay with women who assembled at the door of the tabernacle of meeting." In other words, they were fornicating with women as they entered the sanctuary. Can you imagine? That would be like the pastor's sons having sex with members of the church behind the building. Actually, more blatant: in the front lobby.

Just as members of the congregation warned Sammy's pastors that he was sinning, the people of Israel warned Eli that his sons were sinning. Just as Sammy's pastors did nothing more than have a talk with him, Eli did nothing more than have a talk with his sons. He said to them:

> "Why do you do such things? For I hear of your evil dealings from all people. No, my sons! For it is not a good report that I hear. You make the LORD's people transgress. If one man sins against another, God will judge him. But if a man sins against the LORD, who will intercede for him?"
>
> 1 Samuel 2:23–25

The Bible says that Eli honored his sons more than God. His sons became his idols. The Bible also says that Eli's sons did not heed the voice of their father because the Lord desired to kill them. Eli's idolatry and his son's sexual immorality brought God's judgment on them all.

A prophet spoke these words from God to Eli. Even though his sons would die, God would bless his family. This was likely fulfilled by Zadoc, of the family of Eleazar, in the beginning of King Solomon's reign:

> "Now this shall be a sign to you that will come upon your two sons, on Hophni and Phinehas: in one day they shall die, both of them. Then I will raise up for Myself a faithful priest who shall do according to what is in My heart and in My mind."
>
> 1 Samuel 2:34–35

A Word Famine

Eli was not the only spiritual leader we read about in the Bible who tolerated Jezebel. We have been studying the strong control the spirit of Jezebel maintained in Ahab's kingdom. Ahab allowed his queen to bring Baal and Asherah worship into Israel. These cults practiced perverted forms of worship and prostitution, homosexuality and human sacrifice of children. If Ahab goes down in Bible history as the king who did more to provoke the Lord than any other king (see 1 Kings 16:33), it is probably safe to conclude that Queen Jezebel did more to provoke the Lord than any other queen.

During this wicked reign, famine struck the land of Israel. The prophet Elijah prayed fervently that it would not rain, and for three and a half years, it did not (see James 5:17). It was only after the people of Israel turned back to the Lord—after Elijah's prophetic showdown on Mount Carmel with the false prophets—that the drought ended.

But there is perhaps a more dangerous famine in the last days: a famine of hearing the words of the Lord. Amos prophesied: "'Behold, the days are coming,' says the Lord GOD, 'that I will send a famine on the land, not a famine of bread, nor a thirst for water, but of hearing the words of the Lord'" (Amos 8:11).

This verse speaks of spiritual famine. Although there are pockets of revival springing up around the world, there is also a great famine of hearing the words of our Lord in many parts of the world. That is not because God is not sending His Word, but because people do not want to hear the purified Word of God. Paul said it best:

> For the time will come when they will not endure sound doctrine,
> but according to their own desires, because they have itching

ears, they will heap up for themselves teachers; and they will turn their ears away from the truth, and be turned aside to fables.

2 Timothy 4:3–4

Jezebel has plenty of fables to tell to those who are willing to listen. In fact, this spirit executes its agenda through false prophetic utterances. As we have noted, the New Testament Jezebel called herself a prophetess. Someone tapping in to the spirit of Jezebel can be fairly accurate in giving prophetic words because the prophecies come out of the forbidden realm of familiar spirits or the idolatry in that one's heart. The Jezebelite may utter a prophecy that blends a word of knowledge with flattery, such as: "The Lord shows me you have been hurt in the past, but He is sending reinforcements now into your life to strengthen you. The people around you may not acknowledge or accept it, but you are going to have a widespread ministry."

We are all listening to somebody. We are listening either to the Holy Spirit or to another spirit. And whom we listen to influences the course of our lives. Too many believers are unwittingly listening to Jezebel. They are accepting her teachings that it is okay to serve idols and compromise sexually.

Jezebel might say something like this, "You work hard all week. You deserve your idols. You deserve a little pleasure. It's okay to be greedy. After all, you earned your money and you should spend it any way you want. It's okay to flirt with your neighbor. A little flirting doesn't harm anybody. It's okay to sin, because you can repent later. It's all under the blood."

God forbid!

Jezebel's Murderous Motive

Jezebel is the master of subtlety. You might not even hear the voice. It might just be a slight pulling away from fellowship with God and into the arms of the seductress. I assure you, the end is death. When any believer falls into the depths of Satan to the point that the Lord takes him to heaven early in order to preserve his eternal fate, Jezebel has achieved a measure of its murderous plan. That is one more saint who is not spreading the Gospel of Jesus Christ.

Yes, there are cases in which Jesus will allow the enemy to affect people's lives through sickness in order to get their attention. Jesus does this because He loves them and is trying to open their eyes to their need for repentance. When people repent, Jesus can free them from demonic oppression in a heartbeat.

The Holy Spirit tries many ways to reach people before He allows the enemy to touch their lives at this level. But because He is a loving God with an eternal view, He will let the devil wreak his havoc if they will not repent any other way. That sickness could lead eventually to death.

Again, the goal is to prevent the believer from falling away from the faith, which Paul offers as a sign of the last days.

Remember Ananias and Sapphira? Many in the early Church were selling their possessions and giving the earnings to the apostles to distribute to believers in need. This deceitful couple sold a piece of land and pretended that they were giving the full purchase price to the apostles. Peter asked Ananias why Satan had filled his heart to lie to the Holy Spirit by pretending he had given all the money to the church. Ananias heard those words and fell dead. Later that day, his wife also fell dead in her lie (see Acts 5).

Essentially, this couple was mocking God and deceiving the church. They put other gods before Christ. Money and prestige were their idols. We do not know what would have happened if Ananias and Sapphira had repented. But they did not repent, and the judgment of God fell on them.

Likewise, an unrepentant believer in the church at Corinth met with God's judgment. Paul heard that there was sexual immorality in the church: A man was sleeping with his father's wife. The church leadership was not dealing with it. Rather, they were boasting about the condition of the church.

Paul confronted this behavior: "And you are puffed up, and have not rather mourned, that he who has done this deed might be taken away from you" (1 Corinthians 5:2). Paul judged the sexually immoral congregant, commanding in the name of Jesus that the church deliver the man to Satan for the destruction of his flesh, that his spirit might be saved in the day of the Lord Jesus. Again, see God's motive.

Paul also delivered Hymenaeus and Alexander to Satan so they could be "disciplined [by punishment and learn] not to blaspheme" (1 Timothy 1:20, AMPLIFIED). Paul's intention was that they repent for straying from the faith and return to Jesus. Paul also made it clear that people who take Communion in an unworthy manner eat and drink judgment for themselves:

> For this reason many are weak and sick among you, and many sleep. For if we judge ourselves, we would not be judged. But when we are judged, we are chastened by the Lord, that we may not be condemned with the world.
>
> 1 Corinthians 11:30–32

It was God's judgment that made these believers sick and weak. God was trying to get their attention so they would not spend eternity in hell. Just as Jonah found in Nineveh, true repentance reverses God's judgment.

Judgment: a Manifestation of Love

In the apostle John's recorded revelation of Jesus Christ, which we know as the book of Revelation, Jesus is described this way:

His head and hair were white like wool, as white as snow, and His eyes like a flame of fire; His feet were like fine brass, as if refined in a furnace, and His voice as the sound of many waters; He had in His right hand seven stars, out of His mouth went a sharp two-edged sword, and His countenance was like the sun shining in its strength.

Revelation 1:14–16

Jesus has eyes like a flame of fire—and He sees everything we do. Those eyes can be eyes of fiery love or fiery judgment, depending on what He sees. Never forget that the only reason Jesus releases judgment, or discipline, is because He loves us too much to allow us to travel deeper into the pit of destruction. Ultimately, His discipline of believers is a manifestation of His fiery love.

My son, do not despise or shrink from the chastening of the Lord [His correction by punishment or by subjection to suffering or trial]; neither be weary of or impatient about or loathe or abhor His reproof, for whom the Lord loves He corrects, even as a father corrects the son in whom he delights.

Proverbs 3:11–12, AMPLIFIED

The Lord is relentless in His love for us and although He prefers to pour out blessings of a different kind, He will bless us with discipline if it means saving our souls from Jezebel.

In John's vision, Jesus had feet like brass. Brass is a symbol of judgment against sin. The devil is under our feet—and so is Jezebel. It was Jehu who looked up to the window where the Old Testament Queen Jezebel was watching and commanded the eunuchs to throw her down. "So they threw her down, and some of her blood spattered on the wall and on the horses; and he trampled her underfoot" (2 Kings 9:33).

We are called to trample Jezebel underfoot, which means trampling on the sins that this spirit tries to introduce: idolatry and immorality. Jesus gives us His grace to defeat Jezebel regardless of how subtle are its workings. We have already defeated Jezebel in Christ. We are really just enforcing that victory in our lives by trampling over the sins it promotes. And if others cannot get free on their own, we are called to help. In the next chapter we learn how.

9

Loving Jezebel Back to Jesus

The title of this chapter may strike you as odd. Are we not supposed to root out, pull down, destroy and overthrow Jezebel (see Jeremiah 1:10)? Are we not supposed to wrestle this wicked principality to the ground and run it out of the church on a rail? Are we not supposed to rise up like Jehu and conquer this wickedness? Indeed we are. But much of the Jezebel extremism—and, therefore, deception—in the Spirit-filled Church today happens because overzealous spiritual warriors fail—in the words of that popular phrase once more—to separate the principality from the personality.

In other words, yes, we want to root out, tear down, destroy and overthrow the spirit of Jezebel. Yes, we want to wrestle this principality into submission to the name of Jesus. Yes, we want to charge ahead with a Jehu anointing and defeat this wickedness. But we need to rightly divide between principalities, powers and people or we are just buffeting the air at best and hurting God's people at worst—all while the real Jezebel continues to wreak havoc on the saints.

Far too often even spiritually discerning believers fail to make the distinction between the murderous spirit of Jezebel and a person with a pushy, overbearing demeanor. This happens because we have been trained to spot what the church calls "Jezebel" from a mile away. Generally this involves running down a checklist of traits that may or may not indicate a Jezebel spirit.

I want to start with two examples of false accusation that came from misjudging certain traits, and show how destructive it is—not only for the one being accused but also for the accusers. Misjudging someone as a Jezebel can lead to greater deception in the hearts and minds of those who mistakenly discern Jezebels among them. And that is only a step away from infection by the spirit they claim to be rooting out of the Church.

Misplaced Accusations

It seems more and more that Spirit-filled believers are staying on high alert for Jezebel. And since that is what they are focused on, that is what they find—or at least what they think they find.

Jackie served as a volunteer in a prophetic church for nearly ten years. She ran the children's ministry and was among the largest financial contributors to the congregation. But mostly she was available to do warfare at the pastor's bidding. In time she was welcomed into the inner circle where the senior pastor trusted her with confidential information. If the leadership decided that someone was flowing in a Jezebel spirit, she was among the first to know it. She would then battle against it in spiritual warfare prayer.

Jackie felt privileged for many years; she was often celebrated. Since the church had no money to pay staff, she volunteered her time—up to thirty hours some weeks—while working full-time and raising a son as a single mother. Although the senior pastor's request for her time seemed unreasonable—and although the rules of the church sometimes struck her as legalistic—Jackie was convinced that bowing to the demands of the church leadership was part of picking up her cross and following Jesus. At least that is what they told her.

But she paid a high price for that decision. In the name of building the house of God, Jackie made her son feel second-best for years. He was often sitting in the sanctuary alone while Jackie was working with her team on a prayer project in another room or directing the children's ministry volunteers. Whenever Jackie suggested to the leaders that this was a wrong ordering of priorities, they convinced her to "let go of your son and put him into God's hands." They told Jackie to "just get the ministry work done and trust the Lord with your son."

Jackie grew more and more concerned. But it was not until her son started "cutting"—slicing his arms with razor blades to release emotional pain—that Jackie got the wake-up call she needed. She cut back on her volunteer ministry work.

Jezebel's Abusive Control

The leadership was not happy to lose the many services that Jackie had provided. The senior pastor rebuked her harshly, calling her unstable and saying she was full of fear and rejection.

Those words hurt her deeply, and Jackie buckled down and got back to the work of ministry. But the problem with her son grew worse until one day he pulled out a razor blade during church and cut deeply into his arm in front of several younger children.

Jackie was finally no longer willing to "just get the ministry work done and trust God with your son." She spent time with him alone on Friday and Saturday nights, which meant missing the Friday night service.

And that is when the Jezebel accusation came. Jackie was publicly rebuked in front of the church for putting her family before ministry. She was stunned, but that was not all. Soon, "prophets" in the church began to tell her of their dreams and visions that a Jezebel spirit was superimposed over her body when she spoke. Another claimed a python spirit was leading her into error. Still another claimed she was merciless, unforgiving and prideful. She had been celebrated publicly just months before. Now she was the church villain.

From that point on, during and after Sunday services, Jackie got the cold shoulder. Her remaining responsibilities were handed over to others. Jackie had seen this before. She knew that was the way the leadership shut down a Jezebel. But what hurt Jackie the most was the response from her best friend when Jackie confided that she needed to leave the church. Her friend, fully controlled by this Jezebel-inspired abusive system, called her an uncaring, unloving mother and gave her a laundry list of other false accusations.

The Truth Sets Her Free

When one of the prophets finally said openly that she was "flowing in a Jezebel spirit," Jackie asked for help from other pastors and leaders she worked with outside the church. Jackie asked a prison chaplain she knew if he thought the charge was true. The chaplain answered, "Are you fornicating and leading others into sexual immorality and idolatry?" Her answer was no, and she was able to see that the accusation was false.

Once she understood the truth, Jackie was set free from the wicked words being spoken against her. She was able to war in the spirit against the accuser of the brethren—not the people who made the accusation, but the spirit behind it.

Jackie left that church. When she did, the leaders added to their attack. They preached about how Jezebel was taking people out of the church, making sure that the congregation would know—without their stating it directly—that Jackie was a Jezebel. These pastors also started publishing blog posts and producing You-Tube videos about how Jezebel "takes out believers."

Jackie ended up losing every friend she had in the church, which was every friend she had in the world. But she was free, and her son got into a healthy youth group in a sound church where he started the process of getting free, too.

You see, accusing someone of flowing in a Jezebel spirit is more than accusing someone of being controlling. It is accusing him or her of opposing the Kingdom of God and misleading believers into the depths of Satan. It is a serious charge. People who throw this term around usually need to repent because they are often part of the Jezebel deception.

When church leaders trumpet their ability to root out Jezebel, they rarely see that they have falsely accused a believer. They have hurt a member of the Body. When one part of the Body suffers, every part suffers (see 1 Corinthians 12:26). And Jezebel celebrates.

The Infection Spreads

Although we should exercise spiritual discernment and judge with righteous judgment, we are not supposed to move in a judgmental spirit. Jesus made this clear: "For with what judgment you judge, you will be judged; and with the measure you use, it will be measured back to you" (Matthew 7:2). *The Amplified Bible* says, "Do not judge and criticize and condemn others, so that you may not be judged and criticized and condemned yourselves" (Matthew 7:1). If we have true fear of the Lord, we will not be so quick to condemn someone we think is moving under a Jezebel spirit.

Despite this command, however, I have seen believers with strong personalities be judged—and even condemned—as Jezebels as soon as they walk through the door. They are never allowed to get fully plugged in, never given a chance. Many of these people were merely wounded soldiers with overbearing personalities—not Jezebels at all. Others were type-A personalities with passion to do something for God and a lack of skills to work with people in a graceful way. Instead of helping these individuals grow in the area of tact, the leadership brought more pain by rejecting them from the word hello.

This was the case with Maggie. I will never forget the first time she walked through the door of a small-town church I attended briefly. For starters, she was from a large city and seemed to bring with her a brisk, demanding pace of life, which stood out in the slower, friendly environment of the town. Maggie had a direct and commanding personality that would have been a challenge to most groups; on the other hand, some members of the church were immature and easily threatened. Because of a number of stark differences between them, when Maggie walked into that congregation, the scene was already set for personality conflicts.

Maggie and the church administrator, Betty, clashed immediately. Betty, a new believer who was insecure in her role and her identity in Christ, pegged Maggie as a Jezebel after the first service—the first service! Betty continued to sow seeds with the pastorate and staff about Maggie's Jezebelic tendencies until most were convinced that she was an assignment against the church.

Despite the odds stacked against her, Maggie was a mature believer and continued to push for an opening to serve. She tried at every opportunity—but she always had the door slammed in her face. She became frustrated, and Betty took that frustration as an opportunity to continue building the "Jezebel" case against her.

After three years of faithful attendance and willingness to serve, Maggie realized she would not be offered any opportunities— they would not even let her speak in the prayer meetings—and left the church in proper order. When she did, the staff celebrated because Jezebel was gone. They rejoiced that they had rooted out Jezebel.

But Maggie was never the Jezebel. Betty was actually the Jezebelic gatekeeper who was too threatened to let anyone she could not control have an opportunity to serve. We can thank God whenever believers who are being misjudged get out of these abusive churches and get planted in healthy churches where they can serve the Lord faithfully.

Labeling someone a Jezebel is far more serious than we might realize. And failing to walk in love in an effort to restore a true Jezebelic believer also grieves the Holy Spirit. On the one hand, many in the Church are completely ignorant of the Jezebel spirit. On the other hand, too many blood-bought believers are falsely labeled Jezebels. I know of a church where it seems that every tenth person who walks through the door is a "Jezebel."

But even if a person is controlling—or immoral or idolatrous for that matter—should not the Church be working to restore the believer to God's heart with a spirit of gentleness? Remember, Jesus was patient with the Revelation 2 Jezebel before finally promising judgment. Jesus gave that woman space to repent. God's will is to restore. Should ours not be the same?

Roots and Results of False Accusation

False accusations are often rooted in the accuser's own personal insecurities. Perhaps the worship leader sees a talented young singer rising up and winning the attention of the congregation. Rather than encouraging her and giving her an opportunity to shine, the insecure worship leader tries to undermine the young talent by sowing seeds of Jezebelic accusations against her with the leadership. Meanwhile, others who are truly flowing in a spirit of Jezebel are allowed to run free in the church with titles and honors that they did not earn and do not deserve. It is a paradox that grieves the Holy Spirit.

The Bible says, "Do not grieve the Holy Spirit of God [do not offend or vex or sadden Him]" (Ephesians 4:30, AMPLIFIED). The Holy Spirit is the Spirit of truth. Satan is the father of lies and the accuser of the brethren. Believers who make false accusations against other believers offend, vex or sadden the Holy Spirit. And might it be possible that continually making false Jezebel accusations against our brothers and sisters in Christ could so badly grieve the Holy Spirit that, in His absence, the accuser's discernment becomes contaminated? Could making false Jezebel accusations cause someone not to see the real Jezebel when it rises in that person's midst? We saw this happen in the stories above.

Some believers are bitter against this spirit of Jezebel because they claim, "Jezebel stole my inheritance" or "Jezebel ruined my marriage." That may be true. But the experience may have left them with hurts and wounds so deep that they unknowingly started cooperating with Jezebel to hurt others. They run the risk of making false Jezebel accusations when they themselves are actually the ones infected. If you pay close attention to people who are on a witch hunt for Jezebel, you often see Jezebelic tendencies in them, along with traces of hurt and rejection. That is why forgiveness is so important.

Before Paul warned the believers at Ephesus not to grieve the Holy Spirit, he said, "Let no corrupt word proceed out of your mouth, but what is good for necessary edification, that it may impart grace to the hearers" (Ephesians 4:29). And after Paul warned them not to grieve the Holy Spirit, he said, "Let all bitterness, wrath, anger, clamor, and evil speaking be put away from you, with all malice. And be kind to one another, tenderhearted, forgiving one another, just as God in Christ forgave you" (Ephesians 4:31–32).

Love believes the best, and does not jump to conclusions based on what shows on the surface. The Bible does not have much good to say about presumption. If we walk in love and remain prayerful, though, I believe the Holy Spirit will show us who is infected with Jezebel and how to help them break free.

Restoring Jezebel

The point is this: Even if someone is operating in a spirit of Jezebel, our first aim as believers is to restore the individual—not condemn him or her. If a wounded believer, one whom Jezebel has taken captive, cannot rely on the people of God for help in escaping a bondage he or she cannot see, how will that person ever get free?

Jezebelites can be restored. We will talk more about the practical ministry aspects of setting the captives free in chapters 10 and 11. But let me tell you Kassie's story to demonstrate how to love a Jezebelite back to Jesus.

Kassie was a talented medical professional with a huge heart for underprivileged kids. But a series of devastating events—including her husband dying after a long and painful battle with cancer, losing all her worldly possessions after a partner in the medical practice committed fraud and almost losing her children—Kassie became bitter. She was angry with God Himself—but she never stopped serving in the church. In fact, Kassie, who had been good friends with the pastors for many years, was a key leader.

Although people marveled initially at her spiritual strength in weathering several life-altering storms, Kassie was not as strong as she looked. She had merely buried her emotions and plowed on, never dealing with the pain of loss or betrayal.

The truth was, Kassie felt helpless and out of control. She vowed in her heart never to allow anyone the upper hand in any type of relationship again. That vow opened the door to Jezebel's control. Before long, Kassie's once gentle demeanor turned sarcastic and hard. She began dating a man who was not a Christian and was on the verge of immorality when her pastors confronted her with the uncomfortable truth that they discerned: The spirit of Jezebel was influencing her actions.

Rather than stripping Kassie of what she had left—her work with the children—the pastors began gently counseling her through the hurts and wounds she had endured at the hand of the enemy. Rather than avoiding her like the plague, the staff rallied around her, spent more time with her and committed to pray with her. The pastors kept a close eye on Kassie—not because they were scrutinizing her every move, but because they were looking for opportunities to encourage her.

After several months of counseling, Kassie had a break-through. She forgave God. She forgave herself. She forgave her dead husband for dying. She forgave her partners in the medical practice for ruining her financially. She forgave everyone she could think of. The Holy Spirit then reminded her of the vow she had made with Jezebel. She renounced it, repented before God and was set free. Today, she is more loving and caring than ever because she understands what it is like to be in bondage—and what it is like to be set free.

Not everyone whom Jezebel targets is bound by unforgive-ness and bitterness. Some are bound by rejection. Others are bound by childhood sexual abuse or adult rape. Still others are bound by pride. But it does not matter what the strongman is. Love—not suspicion, accusation or gossip—is always the first step toward setting people free. Kassie's story and many oth-ers like it prove that you really can love people out of Jezebel's clutches and back into Jesus' arms.

Speaking the Truth in Love

If you read beyond the equipping verse of Ephesians 4:11, which has become a mantra of the apostolic movement, you see that unity is the goal. Jezebel opposes this by tossing people to and fro with its doctrines, trickery, craftiness and deceitful plotting (see Ephesians 4:14). We are supposed to demonstrate the love of Christ, even to one who is flowing in a Jezebel spirit. We are supposed to speak the truth in love so that we

> may grow up in all things into Him who is the head—Christ— from whom the whole body, joined and knit together by what every joint supplies, according to the effective working by which every part does its share, causes growth of the body for the edifying of itself in love.
>
> Ephesians 4:15–16

Jesus has given us the ministry of reconciliation (see 2 Corinthians 5:18). Restoration should be our goal—and restoration in the right spirit. Paul told the Galatians:

> Brethren, if a man is overtaken in any trespass, you who are spiritual restore such a one in a spirit of gentleness, considering yourself lest you also be tempted. Bear one another's burdens, and so fulfill the law of Christ. For if anyone thinks himself to be something, when he is nothing, he deceives himself.
>
> Galatians 6:1–3

We see far too little of Paul's Holy Spirit-inspired advice practiced in the Body of Christ. At one extreme, we have mega-church preachers taking narcotics to self-medicate their emotional pain and dying of overdoses. The masses ignored signs of trouble because the church was growing. We see high-profile leaders having homosexual affairs and settling out of court after having lawsuits brought against them. We see pride and presumption on the platform as men of God are carried around in chairs by an entourage, literally. Jezebel is often behind these sorts of acts. No one spoke the truth in love before Jezebel carved a path all the way into the pit of hell for the sake of idolatry and greed.

At the other extreme, we see spiritual hunters who take pleasure in marking another notch on their belts every time they run another "Jezebel" out of their churches. In churches that are actually run by true Jezebelites, discerning believers who suggest there is a problem become the problem and are persecuted until they leave. Sincere believers are wounded by Jezebel's false accusations against them, wondering if the fiery darts of accusation are true.

But the writing is on the wall: If a man is overtaken in any trespass—including flowing in a Jezebel spirit—those who are spiritual are charged with attempting to restore that person in a spirit of gentleness, considering themselves so that they are not also tempted. In other words, it is our job as Christians to love Jezebels back to Jesus, not act like Jezebel and try to control their behavior or—equally grievous—promote them to positions of honor.

God Is Calling Deliverers

People who have been seduced by Jezebel need help to break free. Too often they receive only judgment. Rather than labeling them as beyond hope and trying to get them out of the Church, we should be trying to lead them to repentance with God's manifest kindness, even while we take authority over the enemy in the name of Jesus.

Think about a biblical precedent for a minute. Would King David label one of his soldiers as an Amalekite (an enemy) just because he fell into the Amalekites' trap? Would David turn his back on one of his soldiers taken captive by the Hittites or the Amorites or some other enemy? Or would he send in reinforcements to rescue him?

We know what he would do. When the Amalekites took captive the wives and children of his soldiers, David strengthened himself in the Lord and inquired whether or not he should pursue them. The Lord's answer: "Pursue, for you shall surely overtake them and without fail recover all" (1 Samuel 30:8). Just as the Lord said, David recovered all. But he had to engage in warfare with the enemy to do it. He could not expect his two wives to walk out of the enemy's camp without help. His wives, and the others being held captive, needed someone who was free and strong to help them escape.

A true general in God's army does not sit by and allow the enemy to take his men captive—and he does not leave them captive when they fall into the snare of the enemy. Neither should members of the Body—pastors and congregants alike. If we want to rescue believers from the clutches of Jezebel, we need to go to war with the principality that is binding them—not with the personality in our midst. (We will learn more about this in chapter 11.) We need to walk in love with the one manifesting Jezebelic tendencies and gently restore him or her. That is not always an overnight process. It is not always as simple as casting a devil out. There is often a fortress in one's mind. The Jezebelic believer needs to recognize the stronghold, renounce it, repent—and then deliverance comes.

Even after Abram and Lot parted ways—and even though strife caused the split and even though Lot took the better part of the valley—Abram ran to the aid of his nephew as soon as he heard that the enemy had captured him. Abram armed 318 trained servants who were born in his own house, and rescued Lot (see Genesis 14:1–16). Abram was willing to put himself and his men in the line of enemy fire to rescue someone who had behaved selfishly.

How many of us are willing to put ourselves in the line of Jezebel's fire to rescue someone who is in bondage to this spirit?

It is so much easier to run it out of the church. But that is not God's way.

Setting Jezebel's Captives Free

Walking through the restoration process with someone flowing in a Jezebel spirit takes faith and patience. And some cases are harder than others. But just as it is not God's will that any should perish, it is also not God's will that any should be left in the enemy's camp. Jesus needs humble believers who refuse to judge a person's heart and are willing to rescue the captives. Remember, God rescued stubborn Jonah from the belly of a whale after he repented. Here are some steps to help you.

If the individual will undergo counseling, that is an excellent first step. If that is not feasible, friends who are good listeners can also help the Jezebelite get to the root issues. Out of the abundance of the heart the mouth speaks. As Jezebel's victim discusses people and events, you can discern by the Holy Spirit the root that Jezebel is feeding on.

Once you have identified the root, you can help the person see in Scripture how it goes against God's heart. If the root is rejection, for example, show the person Scriptures about the love and acceptance of God. Arm this individual with a list of verses to meditate on, to begin to renew his or her mind. Whatever the root is, the Word of God can dislodge it from this person's soul. By studying the Word of God in these weak areas, the individual can keep Jezebel from wielding control in her life.

Once the stronghold has been revealed, and the Word of God is being applied, look next for any inner vows. Generally, those who are in Jezebel's snare got there because of hurts or wounds that left them vowing never to be vulnerable again. Such vows invite Jezebel to enter and serve as their "protector."

Look for any signs of rebellion, bitterness or unforgiveness that might indicate vows. These vows must be broken. This step goes hand in hand with forgiveness of those who cause the hurts, and verbally breaking any soul ties—unholy bonds—with them.

Deliverance ministry might be needed in order to cast out spirits of rejection, rebellion, bitterness and unforgiveness. It is also possible that the Jezebel spirit runs through the family line as a generational curse. This curse can be broken by confession of any sin that the Holy Spirit reveals in the family line and repentance by a family member.

Sometimes the conscience of a Jezebelite is so seared that it requires many believers with a great deal of patience to become the gentle voice of the Holy Spirit in the individual's life so he or she can see clearly again and come before the Lord in repentance. When the apostle Paul called out the church at Corinth for its sins, he first regretted making them sorrowful. But he soon changed his view when he saw the fruit of repentance.

> For I perceive that the same epistle made you sorry, though only for a while. Now I rejoice, not that you were made sorry, but that your sorrow led to repentance. For you were made sorry in a godly manner, that you might suffer loss from us in nothing. For godly sorrow produces repentance leading to salvation, not to be regretted; but the sorrow of the world produces death. For observe this very thing, that you sorrowed in a godly manner: What diligence it produced in you, what clearing of yourselves, what indignation, what fear, what vehement desire, what zeal, what vindication! In all things you proved yourselves to be clear in this matter.
>
> 2 Corinthians 7:8–11

Do you see the progression from godly sorrow to repentance? Godly sorrow produces the diligence to war against the spirit that is holding someone in bondage. Godly sorrow produces righteous indignation against the enemy that deceived the Jezebelite. Godly sorry produces greater fear of the Lord that allows Him ultimately to free that individual from the spirit. That is deliverance. But it all starts with godly sorrow, and godly sorrow does not come to the Jezebelite unless the Holy Spirit convicts him or her.

Letting Go

Sadly, there are times when you simply cannot help another person. Just as not every person will be saved, not every person will be delivered from the Jezebel spirit. If the person is not willing to renounce and repent, Jezebel maintains its rights to work through him or her.

If the soldier does not want to leave the enemy's camp—if he truly switches allegiance—then there comes a time to walk away from him. We have to remember that the spirit—not the person—is the enemy. And the Lord is faithful to rescue those who cry out to Him. Psalm 136:24 declares that God has "rescued us from our enemies, for His mercy endures forever." Indeed, "The Lord is near to those who have a broken heart, and saves such as have a contrite spirit" (Psalm 34:18).

The goal regarding someone who falls into sin should be to offer forgiveness and restoration. And that includes someone Jezebel has overtaken. But if the Jezebelite will not stop committing sin in the midst of the Body of Christ and is leading others into sin, then the person has to be removed from the congregation. You will recall that when sexual immorality manifested in the Corinthian church—a man had sexual relations with his father's wife—Paul instructed the leadership to deliver him to Satan for the destruction of the flesh, that his spirit might be saved in the day of the Lord Jesus.

The Final Word

Simon, a false prophet named in the New Testament, reminds me of Jezebel, and is an example of how to deal with a Jezebel in your midst. Let's listen in:

> But there was a certain man called Simon, who previously practiced sorcery in the city and astonished the people of Samaria, claiming that he was someone great, to whom they all gave heed, from the least to the greatest, saying, "This man is the great power of God." And they heeded him because he had astonished them with his sorceries for a long time.
>
> Acts 8:8–11

In the book of Revelation, it appears that the woman Jezebel was a prominent teacher in the church. She was regarded as a prophetess and the people were heeding her words. Like Simon, Jezebel tends to gain attention through her spiritual gifts. Jezebel may even be saved and filled with the Holy Ghost. Simon was. Simon got saved under Philip's ministry and was baptized in the Holy Spirit. What goes wrong? Jezebel lures these people into idolatry.

Although he was saved and filled with the Spirit, Simon was not willing to give up his prominence in the community. As soon as he received the gift of salvation, it was no longer appropriate for him to practice his sorcery. But when he saw that the apostles laid their hands on people who then got filled with the Holy Spirit, he had what he thought was a bright idea. He offered them money saying, "Give me this power also, that anyone on whom I lay hands may receive the Holy Spirit" (Acts 8:19).

What was the root of Simon's quest to use the power of God in the wrong way? Peter said his heart was not right in the sight of God. Simon still wanted people to idolize him just as he idolized power—but this false prophet did not seduce Peter. Thank God, Peter was not enticed by money. He did not even have to go pray about it. Peter said to him, "Your money perish with you, because you thought that the gift of God could be purchased with money!" (Acts 8:20). Strong words.

Simon's story shows us that someone can be saved and filled with the Holy Ghost and his heart still not be right in the sight of God. This should come as no surprise, really, because the Bible says the heart is deceitful above all things (see Jeremiah 17:9). When our spirits are saved, we do not automatically have a renewed mind. The Holy Ghost regenerates us. We change from glory to glory. But we can still carry baggage from our past, and that baggage may include Jezebelic tendencies.

Peter did not just try to get Simon out of the way—out of the church—so he could move on and deceive others. He confronted the spirit. Peter said, "Repent therefore of this your wickedness, and pray God if perhaps the thought of your heart may be forgiven you. For I see that you are poisoned by bitterness and bound by iniquity" (Acts 8:22–23).

The false prophet should be confronted in love and offered a chance to repent just like everyone else. If false prophets and Jezebels will not repent after you have walked in love patiently for a season, the only option is to guard the church from their influence. Jesus gave us His authority. He expects us to use it.

10

Authority Over the Nations

Some promises are fulfilled in eternity. But I believe we can walk in some measure of eternal promises even before we trade our corruptible bodies for incorruptible glory—and I believe the promise Jesus made to those who overcome Jezebel is one of them.

You might call it a down payment on the eternal reward; a blessing for enduring the demonic persecution that may come with resisting Jezebel; a confirmation that Jesus is not a man that He should lie. Here is the promise:

> "And he who overcomes, and keeps My works until the end, to him I will give power over the nations—'He shall rule them with a rod of iron; they shall be dashed to pieces like the potter's vessels'—as I also have received from My Father; and I will give him the morning star."
>
> Revelation 2:26–28

This is the promise to those who overcome Jezebel. The New King James Version uses the word *power*. Other versions use *authority.* Either way, Jesus is promising positions of rulership in the age to come for those who rule their spirits well in the face of Jezebel's destructions. Furthermore, I believe that as we stand and withstand Jezebel in this age, God gives us more authority in our current realm of influence.

Walking in Authority

I am convinced that I am seeing a slight shadow of this promise manifesting in my life even now—and it came after a long battle with Jezebel. For years, I was part of a Christian "organization" (a term I will use here in the interests of privacy) where Jezebel's controlling, fearful, idolatrous, immoral influence reigned in the place of Christ's loving, nurturing, peaceful, godly guidance.

Jezebel's reign was difficult to discern from the outside looking in. (In fact, it was difficult to discern from the *inside* looking in.) Visitors saw, in the organization's leader, an individual who pursued excellence and had a grand vision. But slowly, over time, the Jezebel spirit became more pronounced and the marks of its presence became difficult to ignore.

Performance was put above family needs. "Yes-men" surrounded the organization's leader, who was perched on his pedestal as a godlike figure. Fear and intimidation ran like an undercurrent in the culture. Anyone who did not toe the party line was castrated spiritually. Immorality was common. Integrity was compromised. Spiritual abuse was rampant.

As painful as it was for me to face the reality that Jezebel was actually reigning in an environment where Jezebel was touted as public enemy number one, eventually the Holy Spirit broke through the fog that had settled on my mind, and I started to see Jezebel's fingerprints (and footprints) all around me.

Eventually, needing to assure myself I was not going mad, I sought counsel from a few trusted Christian leaders outside the organization. They were grieved in spirit over the situation. It was hard to face the facts, but I finally accepted the truth that Jezebel had subtly taken over. It was so subtle that—despite the awareness I had of how the Jezebel spirit operates—I was slow to see it. Most of those in leadership of the organization remained unaware of the ditch into which they had fallen.

Confronting Jezebel

When I finally accepted the horrible truth that Jezebel was in charge, I realized that I had two choices: I could pretend I had not seen it and continue in my place of authority there, with all my coveted honors, opportunities, front row seats and dear friends. Or I could be obedient to the revelation the Holy Spirit gave me—and confirmed to me through mature, wise counsel—and walk away.

In other words, I could hang my confidence on the respect I received from the people within the organization, or I could "count all things loss for the excellence of the knowledge of Christ Jesus my Lord," for whom I would suffer the loss of all those things (Philippians 3:8). It was a painful decision, but I chose to count all those things as rubbish, that I might gain Christ and be found in Him at the day of His coming.

Part of the reason why the decision was so agonizing was that I knew I would face tremendous persecution when I left. I had seen others leave Jezebel's den. They were colored with the brush of deception, accused of walking in hurt, wounded-ness, rejection—and even a Jezebel spirit. I did not want to endure that persecution, but I finally decided that I had to obey what the Holy Spirit was showing me or relinquish myself to spiritual delusion. The Holy Spirit had opened a door—and He told me to leave in peace. To stay would have been to disobey. I shudder to think what fate I might have suffered in this age and the age to come had the Holy Spirit not given me the grace to obey.

Just as I feared, when I walked away I was sorely persecuted by the Jezebel spirit working through the very people I had co-labored with for years. Mature believers watching from the outside called it psychological warfare. I learned that you can submit to only one spirit at a time. In other words, you cannot submit to both the Holy Spirit and the Jezebel spirit at the same time. You have to choose. But when you choose the Holy Spirit, God's glory will rest upon you.

My decision to refuse to bow any longer to that Jezebel spirit, and to stop helping that false kingdom advance through efforts I mistakenly thought were serving God, unleashed a war against me that I had never experienced before. After all, the organization had to protect its reputation. Because I was a high-profile member of the group, and because the Holy Spirit did not give me a green light to offer a reason for my departure, all manner of lies were spoken about me. For years I had been a respected teacher within the organization; now I was classified as rebellious, deceived, merciless, prideful—and a Jezebel. It was one of the most confusing periods of my life. I did a lot of soul-searching.

I submitted myself to Christian leaders for examination, and over and over again, I was found "not guilty" of the accusations. And over and over again confirmations came that I had done the right thing. Within months after I left, others started leaving and telling me that they found the courage to escape after I was bold enough to walk away—and walk away without launching a public attack on my accusers (or even responding to their accusations against me). In fact, I was told time and time again that the public attack against me was so vitriolic that it only confirmed for them which party was *really* operating in the wrong spirit.

I say all of this to make a point: Within months of my confronting Jezebel, God began restoring all the things that I gave up in order to follow Him. And not only did He restore them, He gave me positions and opportunities that far surpassed those things from which I had walked away. I could tick down a list for you, but it boils down to authority. Jesus gave me a greater sphere of authority and influence than I could have ever imagined. He began to fulfill prophetic words and dreams from years ago in rapid-fire succession.

Whereas Jezebel tried to shut down my voice by discrediting me, Jesus opened the doors of utterance among the nations. Indeed, this book is part of the manifestation of that promise—and this is only part of the blessing for the persecution I endured at Jezebel's hand. And it never would have been possible if I had not overcome Jezebel with a Jehu anointing that refused to be intimidated.

True or False Authority?

If you are born again, then you have keys to the Kingdom—whatever you bind on earth is bound in heaven, and whatever you loose on earth is loosed in heaven (see Matthew 18:18). If you are born again, you have authority to tread on serpents and scorpions and over all the power of the enemy—and nothing will cause you harm (see Luke 10:19). If you are born again, you have the right to use the name of Jesus, the name above all names, the name at which every knee must bow (see Philippians 2:10).

In other words, you have authority. You have authority because Jesus gave it to you. What you do with that authority is vital. When you use God's Word the way God wills, He is inclined to give you more opportunity. When you do not use God's Word God's way—such as to bring increase to the Kingdom, to comfort those who mourn, to edify people—He is inclined to take those opportunities and give them to someone who ministers His purpose more faithfully. This concept is illustrated in Jesus' Parable of the Sower (see Matthew 13).

Much the same, I believe that when we misuse our authority, or we are not willing to exercise it according to God's will, we open the door to the enemy. Sometimes that enemy is named Jezebel. Jezebel cannot fully accomplish its work in this realm, however, without a physical body. Jezebel wants to use yours and mine to get its dirty work done. Jezebel wants to usurp our authority but cannot do it forcibly. We have to hand our authority over.

We know that all true spiritual authority comes from our loving Jesus. Jezebel, by contrast, walks in false authority— unlawful rulership that it usurps. It was the Old Testament Queen Jezebel who proclaimed to her husband, "You now exercise authority over Israel," and then proceeded to write letters in King Ahab's name, seal them with his seal and send them to do her bidding.

Let me review that episode for you. Ahab was depressed because Naboth would not sell him his vineyard. Jezebel moved on the opportunity to use Ahab's authority. Her letters proclaimed a fast, and gave instructions for Naboth to be seated with high honor among the people. But it was a trap. Jezebel also instructed two men to sit near Naboth and bear false witness against him, saying he had "blasphemed God and the king," and then to kill him. Jezebel's motive for murder was to take possession of the vineyard. Jezebel had to work through Ahab to get her dirty work done. But it is important to note that compliant Ahab was rewarded with what he wanted in the end. (See 1 Kings 21:5–15.)

This betrayal of Naboth was spiritual abuse in its most extreme form, demonstrating the Jezebel spirit's murderous intent. We see it in stories of the prophets of Jehovah as well. If you will not bow down and give the Jezebel spirit what it wants, it will accuse you falsely and destroy your reputation. If you will not prophesy the words of Jezebel, this spirit will work overtime to cut off your voice by putting you in bondage. If you confront Jezebel's wickedness, it will threaten to murder you. True authority relies on the law of God to bring justice where justice is due; Jezebel perverts the law of God to bring judgment where judgment is not due.

True spiritual authority refuses to tolerate the work of the enemy, and refuses to violate the law of love. True authority puts on the whole armor of God to wrestle against principalities and powers, including Jezebel, but never forgets that the armor is more than a sword alone. Righteousness, truth, faith and peace are essential to walking in true spiritual authority. When you compromise in those areas, you compromise your efficacy against principalities and powers. People flowing in a Jezebel spirit walk in false authority—or they abuse the authority they have.

He Who Overcomes

Jesus often shows us the benefit of obeying His commands. He sometimes appeals to our selfish nature, so to speak, by showing us the rewards of obedience. For example, if we give, it will be given to us "pressed down, shaken together, and running over" (Luke 6:38). If we seek first the Kingdom of God and His righteousness, everything else we need will follow (see Matthew 6:33). Jesus' Sermon on the Mount is full of such examples. By forgetting not all His benefits, we find extra motivation to be good and faithful servants. It is the good and faithful servants, after all, who receive greater authority.

Let's look at Jesus' promise from Revelation again with regard to overcoming Jezebel:

"And he who overcomes, and keeps My works until the end, to him I will give power over the nations—'He shall rule them with a rod of iron; they shall be dashed to pieces like the potter's vessels'—as I also have received from My Father; and I will give him the morning star."

Revelation 2:26–28

Jesus expects us to take a stand against the spirit of Jezebel in whatever form it is manifesting, because tolerating even a little bit of Jezebel's influence could eventually lead us all the way down to the pit of darkness. "A little leaven leavens the whole lump" (Galatians 5:9), and it is "the little foxes that spoil the vines" (Song of Solomon 2:15).

Refusing to tolerate Jezebel does not always mean a showdown at Mount Carmel with false prophets. Sometimes it is a matter of the heart. When we stand fast against the destructions coming against us, we receive a measure of these promises of power in our lives now—and much more in the life ahead. To be sure, Jesus has made some monumental promises that surpass anything we will realize in this lifetime. These promises last an eternity. But I believe that meditating on these promises can help us overcome Jezebel's influence.

Consider this: One of the promises to those who overcome Jezebel is power—and that is what those who fall into Jezebel's snare of idolatry are really after in the first place. Often, people fall into the sin of greed, which is idolatry, because they want the power and influence that money can buy. When we are content as co-laborers with Christ, helping to usher the Kingdom to earth as it is in heaven, we walk in God's authority—the power of the Holy Spirit.

Another promise is the bright morning star, which is a greater revelation of Jesus. When we see Jesus for who He is, our relationships with Him grow in intimacy—and intimacy is what people who fall into Jezebel's snare of sexual immorality are really after. Jezebel propagates false authority and false intimacy. Jesus is the way, the truth and the life (see John 14:6).

Millennial Kingdom Authority

Both the Gospels and the epistles give us insight into eternity. Second Timothy 2:12 assures us that if we endure, we will reign with Jesus. This is directly in line with what Jesus told the church at Thyatira about overcoming Jezebel. If we are faithful to walk in Christ no matter how much it costs us, Jesus will reward us in the coming age. If we conform to Christ and die to self, we may suffer in the flesh but we will reign in the spirit.

In the Parable of the Talents, Jesus drove the point home (see Luke 19:11–27). You know the story. A nobleman needed to make a long trip back to headquarters to get authorization for his rule. Before he left, he called ten servants and gave them each one talent with clear instructions to do business until he got back. When he returned, he checked in with the servants to see how they had used the talents.

The first servant earned ten talents more, the second servant earned five talents more, and the third servant buried his talent in the ground. What did the nobleman do? He gave the first servant authority over ten cities. He gave the second servant authority over five cities. And he rebuked the third servant, taking away his talent and giving it to the one with ten talents.

Here is the point in the context of the battle against Jezebel: Jesus has given us everything we need to overcome Jezebel in this age—and to help others overcome. Jesus has given us His authority (see Luke 10:19). He has given us the privilege of praying in His name (see John 14:13). He has given us His armor (see Ephesians 6:10–18). He has blessed us with every spiritual blessing (see Ephesians 1:3). He has made us more than conquerors (see Romans 8:37).

The One who is in us is greater than Jezebel. Jesus is seated at the right hand of the Father, making intercession for us even now (see Hebrews 7:25; 8:1). And the Holy Spirit helps us in our weakness because we do not know how to pray (see Romans 8:26). Here we have two members of the Trinity interceding for us to the Father, who loves us. Think about that for a moment. Let it permeate your soul. If God is for us, who can be against us (see Romans 8:31)?

The only way we can lose the war against Jezebel is to bury all this in the ground and refuse to submit to the Lord's reign. If we submit to Jezebel and its witchcraft, we will meet with judgment. But if we endure, we will reign with Jesus. Jesus said, "To him who overcomes I will grant to sit with Me on My throne, as I also overcame and sat down with My Father on His throne" (Revelation 3:21). We have the written Word of God and we have the Holy Spirit to lead us and guide us into all truth. And that means we have no excuse to allow ourselves to fall headlong into the Jezebel deception.

Measures of Spiritual Authority

Through the Parable of the Talents, it becomes clear that we will have different measures of authority in eternity. When we approach the judgment seat of Christ as born-again believers, we are not at risk of going to hell. We are "fellow citizens with the saints and members of the household of God, having been built on the foundation of the apostles and prophets, Jesus Christ Himself being the chief cornerstone" (Ephesians 2:19–20).

But Paul warned that we have to take heed as to how we build on the foundation:

> For no other foundation can anyone lay than that which is laid, which is Jesus Christ. Now if anyone builds on this foundation with gold, silver, precious stones, wood, hay, straw, each one's

work will become clear; for the Day will declare it, because it will be revealed by fire; and the fire will test each one's work, of what sort it is. If anyone's work which he has built on it endures, he will receive a reward. If anyone's work is burned, he will suffer loss; but he himself will be saved, yet so as through fire.

1 Corinthians 3:10–15

What did Paul mean by this? We need to stay true to the doctrines of Christ. We cannot add to or take away from the Gospel. The Word is inerrant, "like silver tried in a furnace of earth, purified seven times" (Psalm 12:6). We are to build on this foundation of gold, silver and precious stones within His Word. The alternative is building on wood, hay and straw—which means trying to add to Scripture our own revelations, doctrines of man, doctrines of demons and other errors. Some people are building on false doctrines now, even with a sincere heart. This is part of the Jezebel deception. Yet we cannot claim to be victims, because we are victors in Christ.

Consider the conclusion to the Sermon on the Mount:

"Therefore whoever hears these sayings of Mine, and does them, I will liken him to a wise man who built his house on the rock: and the rain descended, the floods came, and the winds blew and beat on that house; and it did not fall, for it was founded on the rock. But everyone who hears these sayings of Mine, and does not do them, will be like a foolish man who built his house on the sand: and the rain descended, the floods came, and the winds blew and beat on that house; and it fell. And great was its fall."

Matthew 7:24–27

God has given us His Word, and He will reward us for keeping it. We will all have different measures of authority. Paul put it this way:

Therefore we make it our aim, whether present or absent, to be well pleasing to Him. For we must all appear before the judgment seat of Christ, that each one may receive the things done in the body, according to what he has done, whether good or bad.

2 Corinthians 5:9–10

We want to hear Jesus say, "Well done, good and faithful servant." And we want to step into our millennial Kingdom rule, which is based on our faithfulness on the earth.

Shunning Immorality

If we are faithful to shun immorality, we will reign with Christ in the Millennium. If we are faithful to shun immorality, we will receive the Morning Star, which is a symbol of the revelation of Jesus and His authority. If we are faithful to shun immorality, we will have greater prophetic insight into the days ahead because our relationship with Him will not be muddied by Jezebel's seduction (see 2 Peter 1:19).

Of course, shunning immorality is not the only measure of our eternal rewards; holiness is the baseline, without which no one shall see the Lord (see Hebrews 12:14). If we suffer with Him, we will also reign with Him (see 2 Timothy 2:12). Jesus said that those who endure to the end will be saved (see Matthew 24:13).

In the book of Acts, the apostles warned their hearers to abstain from sexual immorality (see Acts 15:20). Paul was grieved that sexual immorality was present in the Corinthian church (see 1 Corinthians 5:1). Paul wrote in his epistle to the Corinthians "not to keep company with sexually immoral people" (1 Corinthians 5:9), and went on to make it clear that "the body is not for sexual immorality but for the Lord, and the Lord for the body" (1 Corinthians 6:13).

A few sentences later, Paul warned the church: "Flee sexual immorality. Every sin that a man does is outside the body, but he who commits sexual immorality sins against his own body" (1 Corinthians 6:18). He reminded his readers that the Israelites committed sexual immorality, and in one day 23,000 died (see 1 Corinthians 10:8). Paul went on to tell the Thessalonians that they should abstain from sexual immorality (see 1 Thessalonians 4:3). Jude warned that the people of Sodom and Gomorrah, and the cities around them, gave themselves over to sexual immorality, went after "strange flesh" and suffered "the vengeance of eternal fire" (Jude 1:7). Let us not forget that Jesus told us to shun immorality as a requisite to having authority over the nations.

But here is the point: So long as we limit our definition of Jezebel to a spirit of control, we will be resisting the wrong thing. Jesus does not offer the promise of Revelation 2:26–28 to those who keep a spirit of control from operating in their churches. This promise is to those who resist immorality and idolatry.

Now that we know what Jezebel truly is, we can hold fast to the end to resist the depths of Satan and the destruction it brings. We can speak forth boldly against the true spirit of Jezebel and rescue many from its seduction. And we can rule with Christ in His millennial reign.

Let's look, then, at the keys to freedom.

11

Will the Real Jezebel Please Stand Up?

You have seen the Jezebel deception. You have unraveled the murder mystery through the pages of this book.

Now consider: Would you recognize a true Jezebelite if you saw one? Would you discern the principality operating over a territory? Would you see this spirit influencing your own soul before—or after—you fell prey to it? Or would this seductress still cuckold you? Before you answer that question, read on with a humble heart.

You could say that biblical knowledge is power—but that is true only if it is applied. Without careful application, even the most exhaustive study is merely an exercise in religion. That is why I want to equip you with practical knowledge of how the Jezebel deception applies to your everyday life. In this chapter you will learn how to work with Jesus in order to trample Jezebel under your feet.

Jezebel is not a textbook spirit. This is a real-world battle. I want you to close the pages of this book equipped to discern the operations of Jezebel in any setting, whether it is in your city, in your church, in your friend—or in you.

I am not talking about going on a witch hunt here. Remember, that is part of the Jezebel deception. I am talking about using wisdom and the gift of discerning of spirits to identify Jezebel's operations so that you can take the appropriate measures—in the grace of God—to deal with it.

Principalities Over Cities and Regions

Whether you call them territorial strongholds, territorial spirits or principalities, there are indeed spiritual forces over some cities that seek to forward the devil's agenda. From prostitution to drug addiction to gambling to divination—there are many demonic strategies that distract people from the truth and light of the Gospel, and hinder the will of God from breaking in to a city or region. In fact, principalities rule uncontested in some areas of the world where the Gospel is largely shut out—and that is why the Gospel is largely shut out.

According to Ephesians 6:12, we know that our struggle is not against flesh and blood—it is not against the pimps and drug dealers and witches—but "against principalities, against powers, against the rulers of the darkness of this age, against spiritual hosts of wickedness in the heavenly places." We saw a principality in action in the book of Daniel, which worked to hinder a prayer answer for 21 days (see Daniel 10:13). We know that principalities and powers try to separate people from the love of God in Christ (see Romans 8:38–39). But we also know that Jesus disarmed principalities and powers—"He made a public spectacle of them, triumphing over them" (Colossians 2:15). He is now seated at the right hand of God, "far above all principality and power and might and dominion, and every name that is named" (Ephesians 1:21).

Discerning Jezebel Over Your City

Why does Jezebel reign over some cities and nations? The answer is not profound. Not really. The painful truth is simple: Jesus gave us authority to enforce His victory and the Church has not always exercised that authority, particularly when it comes to Jezebel.

Look at what happened when Queen Jezebel exerted her influence over Old Testament Israel: The voice of the Lord was largely cut off. There was power-motivated murder, lust, spiritual adultery, idolatry, witchcraft and the exaltation of false prophets. Similarly, the New Testament Jezebel taught and seduced believers to worship idols and to follow their lusts. Where Jezebel manifests, there are sexual perversions of all kinds. Sadly, it is often tolerated in our secularist society—sometimes it is even tolerated in the Church.

We often see earmarks of Jezebel's influence over a city in much the same way that there are earmarks of God's influence over a city. There are clues that Jezebel is exerting its seducing influence in a particular region.

Two key steps can help you discern Jezebel over your city, in a process known as spiritual mapping. The first is researching the history of the area to see if certain iniquities occurred there that could have given Jezebel a foothold. But remember that this is just the first step. It is not advisable to try to deduce the presence of Jezebel in a city and launch into spiritual warfare based on facts and figures alone. The information you need to defeat the enemy is best revealed through the second step: prayer, fasting and Holy Ghost revelation as He wills.

Spiritual mapping—the combination of research and prayer—often reveals the demonic strongholds over a territory. It can unlock the secrets of why certain sins seem to dominate in certain locations.

Also notice the natural dynamics. In modern society, a city where Jezebel rules may have a strong presence of psychic houses—palm readers, crystal ball readers, tarot card readers and the like. A city where Jezebel rules may be overflowing with adult entertainment clubs, pornography stores, homosexuality—including bisexuality and transgender sexuality—adultery, abortion and divorce. Although these issues are present in some form in many cities, the marked difference in a city dominated by a Jezebel spirit is the prevalence of these issues.

Let's look at an example. Jezebel has a territorial stronghold in South Florida (the southernmost part of mainland Florida), which is where I live. South Florida is sometimes called the "evangelist's graveyard." In this territory, to use a phrase you may recognize, the heavens seem as hard as bronze. Bronze heavens are part of the curse of the Law (see Deuteronomy 28:23). This makes it seem as though our prayers rise only to hit a bronze ceiling and fall back down to the earth again. Of course, we know that is not true because God hears the prayers of the righteous (see Proverbs 15:8).

How do we see Jezebel manifesting? The Bible talks about rebellion as the sin of witchcraft (see 1 Samuel 15:23). Well, South Florida is home to a cornucopia of cultural rebellion through homosexuality, an active drug scene, indecent nightclubs and the like. The Bible talks about Jezebel and her witchcraft (see 2 Kings 9:22). South Florida is home to a diverse population that has brought Santeria from Cuba, voodoo from Haiti and Rastafari from Jamaica—and God knows what other devils from various other parts of the world. You might say the principalities and powers here are as eclectic as the population.

Statistics confirm Jezebel's manifestation here. Florida ranks second in the percentage of gay, lesbian and bisexual population behind California, according to the U.S. Census Bureau. That is Jezebel's perversion and sexual immorality manifesting. Miami has the highest HIV rates in the United States, also according to the U.S. Census Bureau. That is the fruit of Jezebel's perversion and sexual immorality.

In Miami, the competition among psychics is fierce—and big business. The former co-host of Psychic Friends Network sued the operators of a South Florida Psychic phone line for using its founder's name to promote its own service. A decade ago, the Psychic Readers Network—of Miss Cleo fame—settled a court case with the Federal Trade Commission and paid a $5 million fine. That is the manifestation of Jezebel's idolatry and witchcraft.

The Barna Group reports that Miami is among the top cities in the nation having the fewest self-identified Christians. *Men's Health* identifies Miami as one of the "least religious" cities in America. *Forbes* magazine ranks Miami as the tenth greediest city and the third vainest city in the United States. Overall, *Forbes* ranked Miami the tenth most sinful city in the United States.

That is the fruit of Jezebel's influence over this territory. Although all revelation should come from the Holy Spirit, it can be helpful to understand these sorts of natural dynamics. That can help you see how principalities—including Jezebel—may be influencing the population, and help you know how to pray.

If you are certain that Jezebel is dominating your city, how should you proceed? First, Jezebel is not a principality that you go after alone in your prayer closet. And, second, Jezebel will not relent until Jesus comes back. In other words, even an army of prayer warriors is not going to pull down Jezebel over your city at one church service or conference.

When targeting the Jezebelic influences over your territory, join in a corporate prayer group to bind the spirit's operations—but only by the distinct leading of the Holy Spirit. If you try to tackle Jezebel in the flesh, the enemy will launch a counterattack you may not be expecting—or prepared for.

Ultimately, the best way to send Jezebel packing is by contending for revival until God pours out His Spirit and an awakening occurs that brings sinners and saints alike to their knees. When true revival comes to a city, souls are saved, lives are changed and Jezebel loses its grip on sinners engaged in sexual immorality and idolatry.

Jezebel at the Individual Level

When it comes to dominance by the Jezebel spirit at an individual level, I subscribe to the late Dr. Lester Sumrall's theory of demon possession as outlined in his classic *Demonology & Deliverance, Volume 1**. Dr. Sumrall describes seven stages of demonic influence: regression, repression, suppression, depression, oppression, obsession and possession. These are applicable to the activity of the Jezebel spirit. Keep in mind that it was Sumrall who said the greatest enemy to the end time Church would be the spirit of Jezebel.

I believe that the predominant way Jezebel enters an individual's soul is through hurts and wounds—and the vows (or covenants) that often follow consciously or subconsciously. Many times, those wounds are tied to rejection. I remember lying in my bed weeping one afternoon. I can no longer remember why I was so upset, but I do remember a voice coming to me whispering these words, *I'll never let anyone hurt me like that ever again!*

That was the voice of Jezebel trying to seduce me. Jezebel wanted me to make a covenant with it by taking a vow—one that would position this spirit as a guard over my life to shut out the love of God and invite other demons into my soul. If

---

*Dr. Lester Sumrall, *Demonology & Deliverance* (South Bend, Ind.: LeSEA Publishing Co., 2001), 1:103–117. Copyright © 2001 by LeSEA Publishing Co. Used by permission.

I had repeated those words out of my mouth or even agreed with them in my mind, I would have made a pact with Jezebel that would have given this spirit permission to plague my soul for the rest of my days (or at least until I recognized the need to repent and found deliverance).

By the grace of God, I had a check in my spirit when I heard those words. They startled me. I rose up and rebuked that voice in the name of Jesus, then quickly forgave my enemies, prayed for them and moved on. See, the devil does not fight fair. Jezebel will wound you and then trick you into making a pact with it by a spoken vow, in order "to protect you" from ever being hurt again.

Whenever you make that vow, the demon comes in and the walls go up—walls that shut out the true voice of love. You may not act any differently at first. But when you come across situations that remind you of the hurt you suffered or a particular incident pours salt into that unhealed wound (Jezebel will never heal your wounds, only stir them up for its benefit), you will begin to manifest signs that Jezebel is influencing your thoughts, words and deeds.

Let's look now at the seven degrees of demonic influence, drawing from Sumrall's listing, as related specifically to the Jezebel spirit.

Stage One: Regression

The first step is regression. As it relates to the Jezebel spirit's ability to influence the soul—the mind, will and emotions—this manifests as backsliding into old behavior patterns. Just as someone who has been delivered from alcohol addiction may slide back to the bar to have a drink on a stressful day, the wounded soul who makes a pact with Jezebel will revert to self-protection and self-vindication rather than relying on God for protection and vindication. The good news, Sumrall notes, is that anyone can overcome regression through prayer and praise. And the pact must be broken, of course.

Stage Two: Repression

Stage two is repression. The dictionary defines *repress* as "to put down by force" and "to prevent any natural or normal activity or development." Repression is further defined as "a mental process by which distressing thoughts, memories or impulses that may give rise to anxiety are excluded from consciousness and left to operate in the unconscious."

In this stage, Jezebel puts more pressure on its victim, which can influence the victim's behavior. A once patient and kind person who is repressed by Jezebel may react with anger to a non-threatening situation because it taps in to an old wound. The person being targeted is reminded of the pain, whether consciously or subconsciously, and reacts.

Because of the vow, the individual is led by the spirit of Jezebel rather than the Spirit of God. In other words, rather than manifesting the fruit of the Spirit, the individual manifests the fruit of Jezebel, however subtle. There is the potential for the person to become a Jezebelite at this early stage.

What is the fruit of the Jezebel spirit? At the surface level— and from my practical experience dealing with this spirit—the fruit of the Jezebel spirit includes control, manipulation, flattery, strife, defensiveness, pride, dishonesty, ungratefulness, a critical spirit, overcompetitiveness, intimidation, super-spiritualism, pushiness, attention-seeking, vengefulness, disapproval, over-ambition, independence, disdain for authority, position-seeking, lust, hunger for power and a religious spirit.

Let me add that just because someone manifests one—or even a few—of these signs, we cannot conclude automatically that a Jezebel spirit is at work. Remember, we are not on a witch hunt. These are earmarks of Jezebel, but they are also earmarks of other spiritual wickedness—including mere works of the flesh.

Paul explains,

> Now the works of the flesh are evident, which are: adultery, fornication, uncleanness, lewdness, idolatry, sorcery, hatred, contentions, jealousies, outbursts of wrath, selfish ambitions, dissensions, heresies, envy, murders, drunkenness, revelries, and the like; of which I tell you beforehand, just as I also told you in time past, that those who practice such things will not inherit the kingdom of God.
>
> Galatians 5:19–21

We must rely on the discernment of the Holy Spirit to recognize Jezebel, and we must understand that Jezebel taps in to the appetites of the flesh with its idolatry and immorality.

Stage Three: Suppression

Jezebel's influence becomes more dangerous at stage three: suppression. *Suppress* means "to put down by authority or force, to restrain from a usual course of action." Jezebel wants to restrain the real person and usurp his real personality. *Suppression* is "intentionally excluding from consciousness a thought or feeling." The result? Jezebel works through the individual without his even knowing it. Here, the Jezebelite begins to yield more of his soul to this wicked spirit.

At this stage, the Jezebelite may not even be aware of why he is trying to manipulate a situation with flattery or lies—indeed, he may not even fully realize he is being manipulative. The root of the Jezebelite's pain, never dealt with, has been suppressed in the soul. Jezebel is now lending its own personality to the victim. When the Jezebelite wins friends or gains power or makes progress toward various other goals by criticizing or using information for personal profit, he is reinforcing the "rewards" of partnering with the spirit of Jezebel. Eventually the Jezebelite gives more and more of himself over to this wicked influence by way of learned behavior.

Stage Four: Depression

Depression is an epidemic in today's society. According to the World Health Organization (WHO), depression affects about 121 million people worldwide, and is the leading cause of disability. WHO defines *depression* as "a common mental disorder that presents with depressed mood, loss of interest in pleasure, feelings of guilt or low self-worth, disturbed sleep or appetite, low energy and poor concentration."

Although many people experience depression at one point or another, long-term depression can be associated with an evil spirit—and it could be Jezebel. Jezebel may cause this depression, which includes feelings of inadequacy that can lead to the Jezebelite compensating with a prideful or critical stance. Other times, Jezebel swoops in at a believer's low point to comfort her, usurping her God-given authority in the process.

Remember how depressed King Ahab became when he could not get his way and buy Naboth's vineyard? Ahab returned home sullen and displeased (see 1 Kings 21:4). The Bible says he lay down in his bed, turned away his face and would not eat. Sounds like classic symptoms of depression. When Queen Jezebel took over the matter and secured the property, Ahab came out of his depression, and got up to take possession of the land.

Elijah also fell into depression after his dealings with Queen Jezebel's false prophets. The queen issued a threat: "So let the gods do to me, and more also, if I do not make your life as the life of one of them by tomorrow about this time" (1 Kings 19:2). That sent Elijah running a day's journey into the wilderness. The Bible says he sat down under a broom tree and prayed that he might die: "It is enough! Now, Lord, take my life, for I am no better than my fathers!" (1 Kings 19:4). He felt isolated and felt sorry for himself. Classic symptoms of depression.

Depression is not manifesting solely in the secular world anymore; it is prevalent in the Church. When Christians are depressed, they are more willing to hand their God-given authority over to another—and less likely to oppose the devil's wicked plans. Although Jezebel is not the only culprit—or even the main culprit—in escorting depression into the Church, this spirit will take advantage of a depressed believer. Indeed, the Jezebelite's closest friends are often emotionally unstable people who are all too willing to give up control over situations in their everyday lives.

Stage 5: Oppression

We have all seen natural examples of oppression. To *oppress* means "to crush by abuse of power or authority, to burden spiritually or mentally." Much of world history records the oppression of women through sexism, the oppression of ethnic people groups through racism and the oppression of Christians through religious persecution. Jezebel's oppression falls into the last category. Jezebel worships false gods—and, like Ahab, it wants God's people to worship false gods.

As demonic influence grows stronger over the Jezebelites, we find that Jezebel works to oppress its victims by isolating them from voices of truth. Jezebel may use witchcraft, also known in the Bible as sorcery. *Vine's Expository Dictionary* explains that sorcery, as described in the Bible, signifies primarily the use of medicine, drugs, spells and poisoning:

> In "sorcery," the use of drugs, whether simple or potent, was generally accompanied by incantations and appeals to occult powers, with the provision of various charms, amulets, etc., professedly designed to keep the applicant or patient from the

attention and power of demons, but actually to impress the applicant with the mysterious resources and powers of the sorcerer.

Jezebel oppresses its victims largely through imaginations. Imaginations are demonically inspired thoughts or images. Jezebel's victims might hear whispers about being unworthy or unloved, for instance. If the victims choose to vocalize as truth the imaginations that Jezebel releases, just as happens with vows, the words are given power over their lives. When those imaginations are accepted, they can lead to many negative manifestations, physical and otherwise.

The voice of Jezebel can bring oppressive fear, as it did with Elijah. Oppression can also come through spiritual abuse, such as when those in authority seek to control through an obsessive quest for power. Oppression can also manifest as sickness in our physical bodies, overbearing temptations to sin that seemingly cannot be resisted in the flesh, spiritual apathy, a move toward false religious systems, over-emotionalism in any area or even financial pressures and insomnia.

The good news is this: "God anointed Jesus of Nazareth with the Holy Spirit and with power, who went about doing good and healing all who were oppressed by the devil, for God was with Him" (Acts 10:38). Any believer can break free from Jezebel's oppression—or help others break free—by exercising his or her authority in Christ over Jezebel. But until the common ground with Jezebel is rooted out—until any vows or covenants or imaginations are broken—Jezebel has a right to continue working its witchcrafts in a believer's life. The believer must repent and renounce Jezebel to break free.

Stage 6: Obsession

Have you ever met someone who has a persistent, disturbing preoccupation with an often unreasonable idea or feeling?

A compelling motivation? This is the definition of obsession. Sumrall outlined positive and negative obsessions. An obsession with Jesus and His Word, for example, is a positive obsession. A negative obsession, by contrast, opens the door for destruction in our lives.

A believer with a negative obsession is no longer thinking clearly. Where Jezebel is involved, this is the stage at which the Jezebel deception has taken hold of someone's mind. The Jezebelite is believing a lie and is enslaved to this spirit. When a Jezebel spirit deceives someone, that person begins manifesting high levels of the Jezebel characteristics we discussed earlier. Beyond manipulation and control, this is where Jezebel's influence becomes murderous. Jezebel will influence a person to murder the reputation of others, split churches, abuse believers in the name of Jesus and bring great harm to themselves through addictions, including with drugs and sex.

The obsessed Jezebelite is acting out the will of Jezebel and is too deceived to know it. He may even teach against the Jezebel spirit while flowing in it. At this point, without divine intervention, the Jezebelite needs a Holy Ghost confrontation from another believer and full-fledged deliverance ministry to break free from this spirit's dominance. The Jezebelite also needs ongoing counseling, because Jezebel will not give up just because it has been cast out.

Remember, the Jezebelite has given this spirit permission to enter, perhaps by refusing to forgive someone or by making a vow with Jezebel. The Jezebelite may not know that unforgiveness is present or forget that a vow was made because the hurt or wound happened in his youth and he does not remember the incident. This is one reason why a discerning deliverance minister—along with the believer's own training to hear the voice of God—is so vital.

Stage 7: Possession

There has been plenty of debate over whether or not a Christian can be possessed by a demon. For our discussion, we can acknowledge that there is a vast difference between oppression and possession. Possession implies full control and domination. Personally, I do not think that a believer can be fully and completely possessed by a Jezebel spirit or any other spirit. But that does not mean that it is impossible to find a *churchgoer* who is possessed. Do you see the distinction? Not everyone who walks through the church doors, sings in the choir or serves at the altar rail is a Christian.

As we consider Christians with Jezebel spirits, we remember that we are three-part beings: spirit, soul and body. I believe that Jezebel attacks our souls and our bodies, but cannot dominate our spirits. I do not believe, therefore, that a Christian can be possessed by a Jezebel spirit. At the same time, I have witnessed firsthand the lengths of the influence this principality can have on even the most knowledgeable believers.

Recognizing Jezebel's Brand of Deception

Understanding Jezebel's weapons will help you stop it dead in its tracks every time. Remember this: Jezebel cannot control you until it first seduces you (see 2 Kings 9:30). Jezebel's first move is to get you on its side. The spirit often begins with flattery (insincere compliments). Jezebel's flattery might sound something like this: "You are so wonderful. No one sings the way you do. You should be the worship leader here. I don't know why the pastor doesn't see the gift of God in you."

Jezebel often uses soul ties to ensnare its victims. Jezebel works to forge a bond with you so you will trust and follow it implicitly—and so it can ultimately control your mind and behavior. Jezebel also uses isolation tactics to keep you away from others who can speak truth into your life. Jezebel can work this isolation through fear, intimidation, rejection or fatigue. Remember that Jezebel succeeded in isolating Elijah, who ran away from society into the wilderness and even left his servant behind. Where you find Jezebel, you will usually find its running mates: fear and witchcraft.

On one level, the spirit of Jezebel is like the story of Dr. Jekyll and Mr. Hyde, the fictional tale of a man who changes from a mild-mannered scientist to a homicidal psychopath. In other words, the Jezebel spirit may try to push its agenda gently at first, but if the target does not cooperate, it quickly escalates its evil plot.

Practically speaking, this means that Jezebel's first line is to use you as a vessel or a eunuch. Jezebel wants to flow through you to do its evil work. Again, Jezebel targets those who are rebellious, weak or wounded, and knows how to use deep hurts and wounds to mislead and exploit. But if you will not cooperate with Jezebel's agenda, this spirit will attack you and try to murder your reputation. Jezebel may even accuse you of being a Jezebel to deflect the attention from itself.

Uprooting Jezebel

If the Holy Ghost is showing you that you are using Jezebelic tactics to protect yourself or to get your way—maybe you are manipulating situations by sharing or withholding information from certain people, playing emotional games in relationships to get the upper hand or using sexual innuendos as a tool—you need to repent, renounce that activity, ask and receive forgiveness and ask God to grace you with discernment not to fall prey to Jezebel again.

You also need to look at the inroads Jezebel has into your soul so you can truly walk away from the demon-inspired behavior patterns that are influencing your life and leading you to a dark place. Jesus said Satan had no place in Him (see John 14:30). What could possibly be in you that could allow Jezebel to undermine or even usurp your authority as a king and priest? How could Jezebel find a way to get its seductive hooks into your soul?

Take some time for self-reflection and prayer, and ask yourself (and the Holy Spirit) if you have issues with lust, greed or pride. Jezebel flows in sexual immorality and idolatry—and is proud of it. If you have issues with lust, Jezebel has its hooks in you. If you have issues with greed, you have issues with idolatry (see Colossians 3:5). And, of course, idolatry comes in many forms. If you think that Jezebel cannot deceive you, then you are already deceived.

Are you harboring unresolved hurts and wounds, rebellion, unforgiveness, overblown insecurities, hidden fears or rejection? When we knowingly and willfully walk in rebellion, we open ourselves to Jezebel's influence. It is rebellious to choose not to forgive—and our hurts and wounds will never fully heal until we have released those who hurt and wounded us. Flattery is an effective tool for manipulating you if you have insecurities and hidden fears or rejection. You will want to receive the "kind" words or puffed-up prophecies because you want to believe they are true. Once you take Jezebel's bait, this spirit can manipulate you. Rejection causes many varieties of vulnerabilities. If you walk under the shroud of rejection you probably work overtime to gain approval, and Jezebel with its flattery is often right there to take advantage and put you to work for its wicked tasks.

What about the words of your mouth? Have you made vows or declarations over your life that have given Jezebel a right to serve as your "protector"? Have you unknowingly invited Jezebel to rule and reign in your life rather than submitting to God? As we have discussed, when you say things like, "I'll never let anybody hurt me again" or "I will protect myself from this kind of treatment from now on," you are inviting Jezebel to help you make those words true. God is our defender, our vindicator and our justice-maker. Our vows should come only in service to Him.

Remember, Jezebel does not fight fair. Jezebel takes advantage of us while we are down. Unresolved hurts and wounds—and the bitterness, resentment and unforgiveness that often accompany them—are doorways to deception. We should invite the Holy Spirit to show us anything He wants us to see—especially if we sense something is not well with our souls. It is difficult to ward off Jezebel if you have common ground with Jezebel. You can repent, but you have to truly do so, which means turning in the other direction. Jezebel will find a way back in if you do not slam the doors shut behind you once and for all, and ask the Holy Spirit to help you guard your heart.

Guarding Against Jezebel

What if you are not walking in deception regarding Jezebel but, rather, are trying to guard your heart—or guard your church—against Jezebel's invasion? The answer is not to look for Jezebel behind every doorknob. Remember, that response is out of balance and often allows Jezebel to stay hidden while innocent people are accused falsely.

Ask God to help you develop discernment. Judging prophecy accurately is a vital key to avoiding the trap of Jezebel's false prophetic utterances. The apostle John wrote: "Beloved, do not believe every spirit, but test the spirits, whether they are of God; because many false prophets have gone out into the world" (1 John 4:1).

Be sure not to isolate yourself. Stay plugged in with other stable Christians in a local church. "Let us consider one another in order to stir up love and good works, not forsaking the assembling of ourselves together, as is the manner of some, but exhorting one another, and so much the more as you see the Day approaching" (Hebrews 10:24–25). None of us is called to walk through this life alone. Surrounding yourself with a community of believers will give you the support—and the accountability— you need to guard against Jezebel.

You need a combination of information and revelation to guard against and defeat Jezebel. We have processed a great deal of information in this book. Now be sure to get the revelation you need from the Holy Spirit, or you could hurt someone and miss the real Jezebel assignment against your life or church. Again, the witch hunt mentality is a big part of how the Jezebel deception works. It is a distraction tactic that causes you to focus on the wrong thing, while Jezebel works subtly in your midst.

You are not going to stop Jezebel by rebuking this spirit every morning upon rising or buffeting the air at every prayer meeting. You are not going to guard against Jezebel by binding this spirit every night just in case Jezebel is lurking nearby. Likewise, fasting is helpful in uprooting Jezebel in your own life, but you cannot fast Jezebel out of your local church.

We need to put discernment back into spiritual warfare in order to move effectively against the enemy. There are times to bind and loose, times to rebuke, times to wrestle in spiritual warfare. But ultimately, you stop this spirit's operation in your life only when you obey. When you pray and obey what the Holy Spirit says—when you walk in accordance with the Word of God and are quick to repent—you will dismantle Jezebel's operation.

Walking in Authority

Remember, Ahab *gave* his authority to Jezebel. Jezebel cannot *take* your authority. You have to hand it over. Ignorance that we have authority (or ignorance of submission to proper authority) is one of Jezebel's favorite playgrounds. Jezebel knows you cannot stop it unless you know you can.

Jesus gave His Church His authority, and He gave spiritual leadership authority within the Church. He expects us to exercise our authority for His glory while also submitting to proper authority in the Body of Christ. We cannot be effective in binding Jezebel if we are acting like Jezebel. We must allow all things to be done decently and in order (see 1 Corinthians 14:40) for God is not a God of disorder and confusion (see 1 Corinthians 14:33). God has set a leadership paradigm in the Church, and we must submit to it.

How does Jezebel usurp your authority? Beyond taking vows with this spirit, you hand Jezebel your authority on a silver platter any time you will not stand in your God-ordained role. Put another way, whenever God tells you to do something and you fail to do it, you give up your authority to a spirit that will gladly take your place.

People operating in the spirit of Jezebel identify the needs of their local church leaders and volunteer to fill the gap. That could be in intercession, children's church or some other ministry where the work is great and the laborers are few. Their motives are not pure—they just want the recognition or the control or the visibility or the praise—but they are willing to do the job when no one else will. The pastor, looking for relief from an overwhelming assignment, is glad to have the help.

When your pastor needs you to head up the intercessory prayer team and you know the Holy Spirit is leading you in that direction but your flesh or soul talks you out of it, a Jezebelite may volunteer to step into that role. When the Lord calls you to be a Sunday school teacher but you are too busy for the job, a Jezebelite is often right there to take up the mantle. Because you would not accept the assignment God had for you, Jezebel now has a guard in place over that department. The Jezebelite will start creating his or her own loyal following, usurping the authority of the pastor in that ministry or department.

Walking in humility is key to rightful submission. You cannot be seduced if you are walking in humility, because you know that apart from Him you can do nothing. We need to stand on this word:

> Let this mind be in you which was also in Christ Jesus, who, being in the form of God, did not consider it robbery to be equal with God, but made Himself of no reputation, taking the form of a bondservant, and coming in the likeness of men. And being found in appearance as a man, He humbled Himself and became obedient to the point of death, even the death of the cross.
>
> Philippians 2:5–8

It seems fundamental, but knowing who you are in Christ, knowing your authority in Him, will help you combat Jezebel's attacks. That is because when you know who you are in Christ you can more readily avoid the pitfalls of insecurity, fear and rejection upon which Jezebel feeds.

Acting Like a Conqueror

After you do all this—after you submit yourself to God and to your leaders, after you decide to stand in your role, walk in humility, grasp your identity in Christ and refuse to isolate yourself—even then Jezebel will not automatically run away. Indeed, Jezebel often looks for another opportunity (or a more opportune time) to attack if at first it does not succeed. That is the time to know your authority. When you stand under proper authority, you can rise up like Jehu the Conqueror and conquer this spirit in your life.

Jehu received a divine commission from God to smite the house of Ahab, and he was successful in doing so (see 2 Kings

9). The Old Testament Queen Jezebel is dead, but the spirit that we call by her name is still alive and well today—and Jesus expects us to overcome it. That means we have to run to the battle lines with militant determination. It takes unconquerable faith to defeat Jezebel. When you sense Jezebel's attack against you, rise up in the name of Jesus. Ask the Lord to give you a Jehu anointing. Learn how to recognize Jezebel's onslaught. Keep in mind that Jezebel uses imaginations, fear and witchcraft, and cast down those imaginations. Let perfect love cast out fear. Bind the witchcraft. Remain on the offense, not the defense. Be a doer of the Word, and not a hearer only, deceiving yourself (see James 1:22). Pray fervently. Pray in tongues. Plead the blood. Submit to God. Exercise your spiritual authority in Christ.

You are a spiritual warrior in the King's army. You have the weapons you need to identify Jezebel in your life or in your midst. That may mean engaging in spiritual warfare. That may mean deliverance. That may mean walking in love. Or it may mean walking away. As you go forth in obedience, the Holy Ghost will lead you into the truth you need to know in every confrontation with Jezebel, whether it is in your own mind, in your local church or in the heavens over your territory.

The truth is, Jezebel has already been defeated. It is up to you to enforce the Lord's victory over this principality, this spirit of control, idolatry and immorality. By His grace, you will succeed.

Index

183

Jennifer LeClaire is director of International House of Prayer, Fort Lauderdale Missions Base, and executive pastor of Praise Chapel Hollywood, in Hollywood, Florida.

Jennifer also serves as news editor of *Charisma* magazine. Her work has appeared in a Charisma House book entitled *Understanding the Five-Fold Ministry*, which offers a biblical study of the true purpose of the fivefold ministry, and *The Spiritual Warfare Bible*. Some of Jennifer's work is archived in the Flower Pentecostal Heritage Center museum in Springfield, Missouri.

Jennifer is a prolific author who has written several books, including *The Heart of the Prophetic*, *A Prophet's Heart*, *Fervent Faith*, *Did the Spirit of God Say That?*, *Breakthrough!* and *Doubtless: Faith That Overcomes the World*. Her materials have been translated into Spanish and Korean.

You can find Jennifer online at www.jenniferleclaire.org or on Facebook at facebook.com/propheticbooks.